The Big Trade

The Big Trade

Simple Strategies for Maximum Market Returns

Peter Pham

John Wiley & Sons Singapore Pte. Ltd.

Copyright © 2013 by John Wiley & Sons Singapore Pte. Ltd.

Published by John Wiley & Sons Singapore Pte. Ltd.
1 Fusionopolis Walk, #07-01, Solaris South Tower, Singapore 138628

All rights reserved.

No part of this publication may be reproduced, stored in a retrieval system, or transmitted in any form or by any means, electronic, mechanical, photocopying, recording, scanning, or otherwise, except as expressly permitted by law, without either the prior written permission of the Publisher, or authorization through payment of the appropriate photocopy fee to the Copyright Clearance Center. Requests for permission should be addressed to the Publisher, John Wiley & Sons Singapore Pte. Ltd., 1 Fusionopolis Walk, #07-01, Solaris South Tower, Singapore 138628, tel: 65-6643-8000, fax: 65-6643-8008, e-mail: enquiry@wiley.com.

Limit of Liability/Disclaimer of Warranty: While the publisher and author have used their best efforts in preparing this book, they make no representations or warranties with respect to the accuracy or completeness of the contents of this book and specifically disclaim any implied warranties of merchantability or fitness for a particular purpose. No warranty may be created or extended by sales representatives or written sales materials. The advice and strategies contained herein may not be suitable for your situation. You should consult with a professional where appropriate. Neither the publisher nor the author shall be liable for any damages arising herefrom.

Other Wiley Editorial Offices

John Wiley & Sons, 111 River Street, Hoboken, NJ 07030, USA
John Wiley & Sons, The Atrium, Southern Gate, Chichester, West Sussex, P019 8SQ, United Kingdom
John Wiley& Sons (Canada) Ltd., 5353 Dundas Street West, Suite 400, Toronto, Ontario, M9B 6HB, Canada
John Wiley& Sons Australia Ltd., 42 McDougall Street, Milton, Queensland 4064, Australia
Wiley-VCH, Boschstrasse 12, D-69469 Weinheim, Germany

ISBN 978-1-118-49895-8 (Hardcover)
ISBN 978-1-118-49896-5 (ePDF)
ISBN 978-1-118-49898-9 (Mobi)
ISBN 978-1-118-49899-6 (ePub)

Typeset in 11.5/14 pt, bembo std by MPS Limited, Chennai, India.
Printed in Singapore by Ho Printer, Singapore.

10 9 8 7 6 5 4 3 2 1

This book is dedicated to all friends and loved ones as well as those who have provided me with support and challenged me to continuously improve, not only as a professional but as a person.

Contents

Acknowledgments xi
Preface xiii

Chapter 1   **Breaking with Tradition**   1
                 Then I Got High   1
                 Training Sequence   5
                 Technical Difficulties   8
                 Reading Is Fundamental   17
                 Inductively Coupled Failure   19
                 The Big Trade   22
                 We're Getting the Band Back Together   23
                 Summary   26

Chapter 2   **The Conditions of Change**   27
                 Livin' on the Edge   27
                 Closing Time   31
                 The Outsiders   36

	Living Day to Day	38
	Sold to the Highest Bidder	42
	Breaking It Down	49
	Finites Move in Infinite Markets	55
	Summary	61
Chapter 3	**Wax On, Wax Off**	**63**
	What Goes Around Comes Around	63
	It's Always Noon Somewhere	71
	Opening Range Jitters	77
	Objects in Motion	84
	Summary	89
Chapter 4	**As the Market Turns . . .**	**91**
	Subconscious Implications	91
	Elephant Walk	95
	Breakouts versus Reversals	98
	Losing Your Inhibitions	100
	Reversal of Fortune	103
	Traders Do It with Frequency	111
	Rules of Engagement	112
	Turn Around and Make Money	116
	Heading for the Exits	119
	Becoming a Reactionary	125
	Summary	126
Chapter 5	**The Range Is Your Friend**	**129**
	Sideways	129
	Waves of Sentimentality	132
	Where Are They Now?	135
	The Edge of Value	137
	The Great One	141
	Summary	143

Chapter 6	Closing Arguments	145
	Crossing the Great Stream	145
	Pressing the Issues	150
	The Point of the Journey Is Not to Arrive	153
	Summary	156

Appendix A Terms and Definitions   **159**

Appendix B Trading Examples   **163**

Appendix C Spreadsheet Examples   **181**

Appendix D Supporting Data for Nvidia Example in Chapter 4   **183**

About the Author   187
Index   189

Acknowledgments

I would like to thank everyone who has an interest in the markets and trading, as you were the inspiration for me to codify my methods and share them with those who are interested in seeking an alternative trading strategy.

I would also like to thank the team at AlphaVN.com, who have risen to the challenge of building something of value from very humble beginnings.

Preface

Over four centuries ago, the invention of both the telescope and microscope brought new focus to a data measurement revolution. The ability to bring far away objects closer and make tiny objects bigger opened the world and sky up to new levels of observation. The science of optics fed our curiosity and ignited our imaginations.

Today our world is awash in data; we are swimming in it. We call this the *Information Age* but we could just as easily call it the *Data Age*. The art of statistics and the use of Big Data are leading to revolutions in fields as diverse as the physical sciences, sports, and economics. It doesn't matter if you're the general manager of a hockey club or a process engineer working for a solar cell manufacturer, data is your work's lifeblood, and without accurate and precise data we would not have been able to make the kinds of strides we have. This use of data is spearheading a decision-making revolution that is changing the very foundations of our society.

Similar to how the use of optic lenses four centuries ago paved the way for the Age of Enlightenment, we are living through a leap forward in the types and quality of observations we can make about our world. No longer are we intuiting our decisions based on a mix of anecdotal evidence and supposition. We can make an observation, test its validity, and make decisions based on it. Data is at the heart of how we conduct business and how prices paid form markets for our goods.

Over the past decade I've had the pleasure to stumble upon this big and small data phenomenon in my pursuit of understanding capital markets. What I have discovered is that data-driven discovery is fundamentally changing the way our lives work, and those who master its manipulation will have an inherent competitive advantage over their peers. This is especially true in the capital markets, where quantitative analysis mixed with the brute force of vast amounts of capital create a very hostile environment for the individual investor. It is my hope that this book will help level that playing field a little bit for you.

As I said, we live in a world steeped in data. Information comes screaming at us in waves and it is easy to be overwhelmed by it, become lost in it. Big Data can and often does overwhelm the smallest actor. But it doesn't have to.

The bigger they are, the harder they fall. One person with an idea and the will to implement it in this age of unprecedented access to high-quality information can disrupt things, and use it to their advantage. Previously, information itself was the barrier to entry into the markets. Today, the biggest worry for most established players is not innovating by producing new information but keeping information under their control and away from you. Think of the music industry or Apple's patent litigation against Samsung and you have an idea of where we're headed.

Take heart, because inside of each of us is our *Big Idea*. I believe that. Everyone has at least one, biding its time and waiting for you to believe in it. With time, attention, and the proper use of Big Data, we all have the means to see our *Big Idea* become real. It's simple, really, when you stop to think about it. It is a little thing in a big world, but it is the secret to finding and making *The Big Trade*.

Chapter 1

Breaking with Tradition

Can you imagine what I would do if I could do all I can?
—*Sun Tzu*

Then I Got High

I don't know about you, but the day I decide to try my hand at something new, it's all I can think about. It's like the smell of a new car. We're not really sure where it comes from or why it affects us; we only know that it does. There's an excitement with any new endeavor. The possibilities seem endless. It is the allure of entrepreneurship, the conscious knowledge that we are taking a risk far outside of ourselves; a leap of faith into the world of potential—and that risk is intoxicating.

In our imagination, making money in the markets looks far easier than eking out a living at our boring day jobs. During the last phase of any bull market, that may actually be true for a lot of people, but sooner or later we must leave the world of imagination and enter the world of reality.

The reality is that valuations of the assets in any bull market—be they stocks, gold, or tulips—become fictional with respect to their fundamentals, and the window of opportunity to recognize that the imaginary world can no longer be sustained is very short and requires swift action. Figure 1.1 shows the spectacular crash of Japan's Nikkei 225 Index, which, if I'd been paying attention, would have served as a harbinger of things to come.

No one puts their money into the market with the intention to lose it. Not one person. But yet so many people do lose. I was one of them. The adage that if you can't spot the fish at

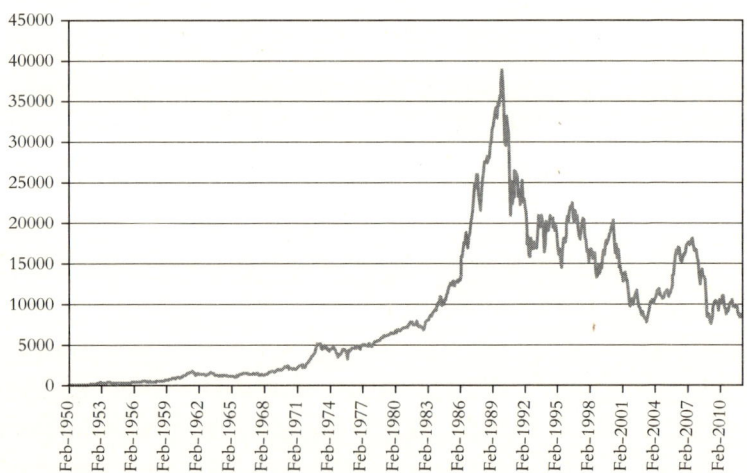

Figure 1.1 Nikkei 225 Bubble
SOURCE: Yahoo! Finance

the poker table, then it's probably you applies very well to the capital markets. Like most people, I sat down at the table thinking that the game was simpler than it appeared, playing against people I didn't know, and expecting to win my first hand. Also working against me was the fact that I had sat down just as the game was approaching its most dangerous moment.

Like many people in 2000, I lost the shirt off my back. When the dust settled and I looked around, I realized that most of the people at the table were fish just like me. Twelve years and a lot of time and dedication later, I see that the landscape is littered with a lot of the same people, still in denial about their lost time and money. They may not be playing the market's equivalent of high-stakes Texas Hold'em (small-cap growth and exploration stocks); they may be putting nickels in pachinko machines (broad market bond and equity funds). But the outcome is the same: They are not being adequately rewarded for their time and capital relative to their needs.

It became my mission in life to no longer be a fish in the markets. Even if I couldn't be a shark, at the least, I wanted to know what the sharks knew so I could anticipate their moves and minimize my risk.

To achieve that goal I had to become an expert in trading, which in my case meant braving the bitter Canadian winter to hit the library and get my hands on the latest books. It also meant finding a new place to live at a time when I had limited means.

When I finished university, I realized the career path I had prepared for was not what I wanted, which meant that I had no formal training or support in my newly chosen field of trading. I knew in my heart that I wanted to live by my wits, investing in the capital markets. My parents, on the other hand, did not understand this and, to put it mildly, disagreed with my major life decision. They were and remain traditional, and it's endemic to Asian cultures to seek a stable and respectable lifestyle. Security is highly valued, and my new plan was the exact opposite of secure. The clash of culture with personal desire reached a breaking point, and I had to find other living arrangements while I focused on another year of intensive self-education about the markets.

I moved in with a friend, Andrew, and effectively lived on his couch while I spent almost all of my time studying. If you have ever seen Steve Jobs's speech from Stanford's 2005 commencement, you will recall that he identified the first major turning point in his life: his decision to drop out of college. In a way, I did something similar. I turned my back on a lot of what I had learned, along with my parents' expectations of me. The comparison ends there, but that part of his speech still resonates with me now.

Capital comes in many forms, one of which is human capital, and my friendship with Andrew turned out to be more important than my monetary savings. Without his support I would not have had the opportunity to leverage my money for my future career in trading.

Anyone who has spent time trading will know that there are as many approaches to it as there are people in the market. While we are all unique, there are behavioral patterns that emerge within markets that can be analyzed to make better-educated guesses about where the price of an asset will go in the future.

I often wonder why the same person who will spend weeks studying and shopping for a new car and engage in ruthless negotiations with the salesman will meekly hand their money over to an investment adviser or fund manager without much thought.

We all have our area of expertise. It is natural to assume that the financial planner is professionally qualified, but those of us who have worked as sell-side analysts know to question that assumption. And you should as well. The fact is that both the car dealer and the financial consultant are salespeople; both are there to close a deal. Financial products are no different than cars; there are good ones and lemons. And just as there are hardworking, insightful financial consultants, there are lazy ones. There are those who spend their days building their base of knowledge and their own systems to distinguish themselves from their peers, and there are those that just regurgitate someone else's work.

By the time you're done reading this book you will not only be able to make your own decisions about specific trading opportunities but also judge the quality of the person presenting that opportunity. And you might decide not to use a financial professional at all.

Training Sequence

It's time that I show you why I'm worth your attention. They say that there is a difference between working hard and working smart. Sometimes when you do the former it winds up being the latter as well. I chose a path that in hindsight was probably crazy, but the risk associated with it and the stress it engendered focused my attention on a singular goal, because anything less would have meant not eating. At the time, I didn't realize that I would put myself in worse straits a few years later—I thought I knew what I was willing to endure to achieve my goals.

All I had to do was figure out how I could consistently make profits by taking advantage of the opportunities the market seemed to present. I needed to figure out how to trade for my dinner. If I could successfully trade for nickels then I could move up to dimes and so on, until eventually I would be trading for amounts of money that would make the time invested worthwhile. In the end, the skills needed to make $20 in the market are the same as they are to make $2,000 or $200,000. The mechanisms by which one enters or exits a trade are the same. The only difference is the size of the position, not the quality of the decision you are making.

The learning process was long and involved. Frankly, I was obsessed with the markets. I needed to figure out how to be not just good, but the very best trader I could be. Pretty much every dollar I made for two years went into this pursuit: books, courses, seminars, you name it. I absorbed it all, tried it all, and failed with a lot of it. As you read through this book you will see me challenge a few decades' worth of collective knowledge with respect to how to analyze the markets.

I'm trying to convince you that I have not come to these conclusions lightly. If you are a technical trader who swears by MACD (moving average convergence/divergence) or *falling wedge breakout* setups, do not think my rejection of them is borne of not being thorough in my examination of their use. Maybe they work for you, but it has been my experience that their reliability is suspect and they can lead someone to make decisions of lower and lower quality over time.

After my first stupid attempt to grab for *the big trade*, I spent way too many nights pacing back and forth, racking my brain to find a better way. If you've been there—if you are one of those people who just can't let the markets exist without you—know that you have a kindred soul. I pursued this life with a singular focus and eventually I began to see a path that did not involve tricking myself into believing in the existence of a trading system built from its foundation that would minimize my confirmation bias and leave me free to make clear decisions with as little emotion as possible.

When I say that I pursued this life with a single-minded purpose I don't think that quite covers it. If you've seen the Christopher Nolan movie *The Prestige*, then you have an inkling of what I put myself through in those couple of years, obsessively devoting everything to becoming the best trader I could possibly be. Sleep was for the uncommitted. Food was a means to continue working, not something to enjoy. The two magicians in the film pursued the absolute limit of their art, driving themselves to catastrophic lengths, the edge of insanity. It made for a great story. It not only resonated with me, but also served as a warning that knowledge is itself a form of trap that can easily lead you down paths that are not true—sleights of mind, as it were.

I'm not going to tell you that I was insane or that's what is required to do this well; I'm only saying that this is what I did. Those around me feared for my health, both mental and physical. They worried that I was working myself too hard, but it didn't matter to me. If you love something and are lucky enough to identify your passion in your life early like I did (and for that I am very lucky), and also have the opportunity to pursue it, wouldn't you? Did I do so without cost? Of course not; there is cost to everything, but it's what I wanted more than anything else.

Having spent literally thousands of hours studying all aspects of fundamental and technical analysis, and trading on that knowledge, I feel confident that I have found a system that consistently works for me. In his book *Outliers: The Story of Success*, Malcolm Gladwell makes the argument that to even have a chance at being great at something, you must put in 10,000 hours of work and study into that activity. Even that's no guarantee of success, but rather the precursor for *potential* success. Don't put in those 10,000 hours, and your chance of success drops. Gladwell's argument may not be bulletproof, but it is food for thought. As we'll see later, it may be another way of expressing a process called *implicit learning*, which plays heavily into my proposed trading methodology.

If it didn't work, I wouldn't have written this book. It's that simple. The concepts we will explore can be adapted to fit your personal trading method.

I'm not saying I always execute this system perfectly—I am, after all, human and have some days that are better than others—but it's the goal that matters. Just because you know you can't achieve perfection, does that mean that you shouldn't strive for it? Of course it doesn't. There is an infinite gulf between knowing the path and walking it.

It is the difference between *specification* and *implementation*. By specification I mean the definition of the problem to be solved or process to be executed. This is the starting point for all human endeavors, really. It is the moment of realization that what we are currently doing does not satisfy all of our present needs, leads us to decide to do something about it. It can be as simple as realizing that you're hungry and need to eat, or it can be as complicated as wanting an outbuilding to store your tools in and have a quiet moment to yourself. In both instances, there is a need to be met.

Implementation is a separate process. That's the mechanical part where you act to fix your condition of need. So you then go into the kitchen and make yourself something to eat or set out to procure that toolshed. Now, making yourself a sandwich is a great deal easier than obtaining a building, but they are still feats of engineering of some form. Conflating the definition of the problem with the solution creates confirmation bias as it walls you off from potential courses of action. Political discourse is rife with this, so is economic analysis.

Technical Difficulties

My goal here is not only to provide knowledge but also to dispel a myth, the myth that markets are predictive. They are not. They are probabilistic. My trading methodology revolves around defining and assessing those probabilities based on a stock's past behavior and the distribution of that behavior.

On the one hand, *quantitative analysis* is defined as a method of evaluating securities by analyzing statistics generated by market activity, such as past prices and trading volume. *Technical analysis* (TA), on the other hand, uses charts and other tools to identify patterns that can suggest future activity. A security's intrinsic value is of no interest.

Technical Analysis

An approach to price chart analysis that focuses on interpretation of the chart's formations. It is a catchall phrase that encompasses a wide variety of techniques.

To put it simply, let's watch a man walk down a city street. If he turns left three times in a row, simple TA suggests that when he gets to the next corner, he will again turn left.

Then again, he might turn right.

As such, there are limitations to a positivist approach (one that uses the scientific method) to trading. Knowing this limitation dispels any notion of finding a magic formula or universal cycle to describe the market's future behavior. That doesn't make technical analysis worthless; it is simply not foolproof. Instead, we can use it to build tools that will, using simple arithmetic, help you make educated guesses with a known probability of occurring and adjust your investment strategy.

With that in mind, if you've ever seen an advertisement for a brokerage firm, you have seen them emphasize their trading tools: "Advanced charting tools that will help you trade like a professional," or some such nonsense. Most professionals don't trade. Most are not allowed to because of securities regulations against owning any stock they recommend to you. This creates an emotional disconnect between them and their recommendations. Without skin in the game, how can they feel your pain that results from their bad call?

Selling is harder than buying. So if they aren't selling you trading expertise what are they selling?

They are selling the illusion that you can learn to beat the market with their software and its myriad of tools. They are not selling you anything unique (90 percent of the tools are available free on the Web) except maybe a user interface that will be overwhelming to any novice trader, and therefore utterly useless.

Over the centuries, back as far as ancient China's rice markets, people have been analyzing how price, volume, and time interact to help guide their financial decisions. Whether they settled on using trend lines or chicken entrails, Elliott waves or the distribution of tea leaves, all of these consecutively and/or concurrently, their approaches were designed to help them predict the future. But, as I will argue later, predicting the market is a fool's errand.

At its core, TA is a means of using our brain's amazing ability to recognize patterns, but with that comes a price.

There are two concepts that come from the school of Gestalt psychology that I believe are applicable to trading. They are *reification* and *multistability*.

Reification is the brain's ability to add into a perceived pattern something that is not explicitly there. Figure 1.2 shows us a number of examples where the black shapes imply an object that is not drawn. Our brain is extremely good at filling in such spatial information.

The implied shapes in Figure 1.2 are not there; they are constructs of our minds. The cones and their spacing imply a sphere but the cones themselves are the only things there. Our brains are extremely good at perceiving shapes and patterns, distinguishing the coloration of a bird's feathers or a deer's coat from the background of the trees and leaves of a forest.

Traditional TA is built on this ability to find patterns and shapes within a price and time chart. Our minds want to distill

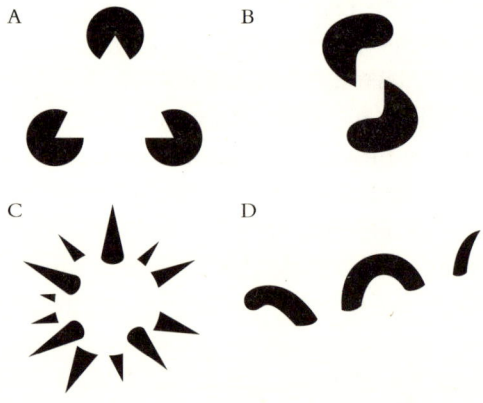

Figure 1.2 Reification (Demonstration in Perception A: Standard Kanizsa Triangle. B: Peter Tse's Volumetric Worm. C: Idesawa's Spiky Sphere. D: Peter Tse's Sea Monster.)
SOURCE: Lehar, S. (2003). *The World in Your Head*, Lawrence Erlbaum, Mahwah, NJ. p. 52, Fig. 3.3 (public domain)

the chaos of the chart down and organize it into something it can understand.

The problem is that the patterns themselves are indicative of nothing. They are just patterns that we have come to recognize and don't necessarily have any significance. In trying to assert that they mean something, we create for ourselves a kind of spatial confirmation bias.

Our brains are trained to look for outliers. It has been shown that a person takes no notice of his habitual surroundings until he perceives a change in it. For example, if you were working at your desk, got up to grab a cup of coffee, and came back to find your mouse was on the left of your keyboard as opposed to the right that would raise an alarm. Immediately, you would begin to try and figure out how or why that happened and it would bother you. I know if I came back to that, I would be suspicious that someone had rummaged through my desk or played a practical joke on me. It would unnerve me for a long time to come, and that space would never feel as comfortable or secure as it did.

This is why a person will get angry when someone cleans up their room without their consent, straightening up their mess. Their mess was catalogued.

Think about how many variations you've seen on the joke about the man who can't find any of his tools after the wife has cleaned up his garage. This is the brain not wanting to relearn and remap that space. Moreover, it will take a long time to adjust to that disruption of routine. The brain is lazy and only wants to incorporate new information into the matrix of existing information, as opposed to constantly starting over again.

> **Tip**
>
> Remove all extraneous markings from your charts, even horizontal bars showing whole dollar amounts (i.e., $10, $11, $12, etc.). Remove all information that is not needed. This is a technique to help you focus.

It makes sense that we would operate that way. Otherwise we would have no ability to discern the important from the trivial, the danger from the routine.

Even if you come at TA with a tabula rasa, not having read a single book or website that goes over the *triangle*, or the *head and shoulders*, or the *wedge*, when you figure them out for yourself, you will find that they are not particularly good at producing consistent outcomes. Rather, you will find that they are at best only guides to future behavior but without the ability to quantify how accurate they are or the extent to which the price can move if the pattern completes.

The first time that a stock fails to perform the way the pattern said it was supposed to, you will begin distrusting it. You will begin looking for confirmatory signals from some other source to help guide your decision, when, in reality, the time may have passed for you to properly make that decision to your benefit. In other words, your opportunity to buy or sell passed you by while you sat around thinking about what to do.

The more this process repeats itself, the more these patterns, which have no tangible predictive value because markets are probabilistic, will take on more *multistable* properties.

Multistability is the process by which our brains cannot distinguish between two interpretations of spatial data. The pattern is equally valid when looked at from two different perspectives; this leads to confusion. The work of M.C. Escher, the brilliant Dutch graphic artist, is rife with multistable images. Figure 1.3 has an excellent example of multistability.

In TA, the pattern itself becomes the focus, not the decision of how to trade off of it. Because your brain can no longer distinguish between the multiple interpretations, it begins to see them all as important.

Everything becomes an outlier.

And, as we already alluded to, outliers are what you should be using to make your decisions.

If you allow yourself to become trapped in an Escher-like maze of false perceptions, you train your brain into a state of

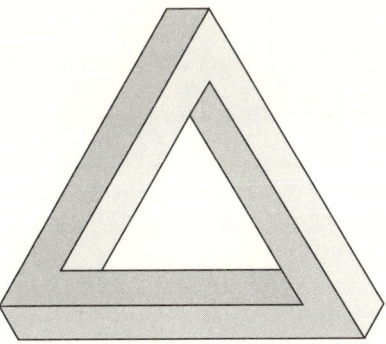

Figure 1.3   Multistability (Penrose Triangle)

hyper-confusion, constantly seeing everything as important. Now, as opposed to knowing that the toilet in your bathroom is in the far corner on the right, you walk into your bathroom convinced that you have to confirm its location. Meanwhile you miss the fact that there is water gushing out of the pipe feeding it, not realizing that until your feet get wet.

It is possible to train yourself into a state of complete paralysis as everything is important and you are trapped furiously trying to catalog it all in real time, which is impossible.

This is why I feel very strongly about simplicity. By not bogging your brain down with too much, it remains free to recognize and absorb information, discern outliers, and recognize and act on them without vacillating between two or more conclusions.

In today's age of information overload, it is easy to fall into this trap, thinking that more information makes you better prepared to trade. As with all things, there is a difference between quantity and quality. With my approach to trading, you are simply looking for the quality information and focusing on the probability that the next tick will be higher or lower than the previous one.

Figure 1.4 is a good example of a chart that would drive a classic formation technician mad. There are no clear signals being given here. One could draw a box around the whole thing, or outline the right half as a broken channel formation, but all of it would be a subjective, multistable interpretation of an asset price

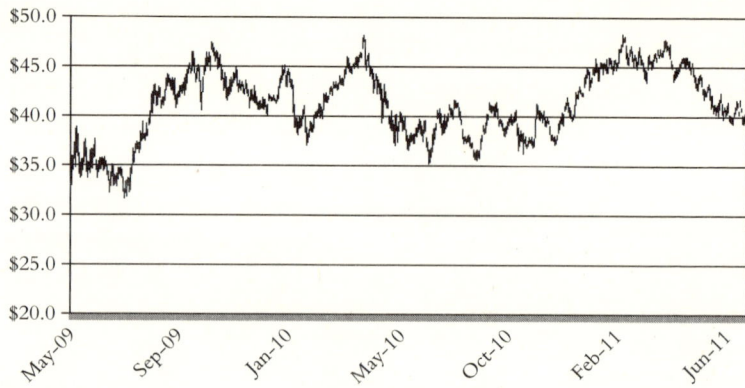

Figure 1.4 Confusing Price Chart (in US$)
SOURCE: Yahoo! Finance

whose current direction is nowhere. At best, one could draw a median line through the whole thing and call that fair value, saying the market is consolidating around that price.

Legendary technical analyst John Murphy has broken down traditional TA using the definitions from statistics:

> The field of statistics makes a distinction between descriptive statistics and inductive statistics. Descriptive statistics refers to the graphical presentation of data, such as the price data on a standard bar chart. Inductive statistics refers to generalizations, predictions, or extrapolations that are inferred from that data. Therefore, the price chart itself comes under the heading of the descriptive, while the analysis technicians perform on that price data falls into the realm of the inductive.[1]

While I may agree with John Murphy that the use of past data to make forecasts of future behavior is grounded in solid

---

[1] Murphy, John, *Technical Analysis of the Financial Markets: A Comprehensive Guide to Trading Methods and Applications*, New York Institute of Finance (1999), p. 18.

statistical theory, the problem I have with traditional technical analysis is that descriptive data sets (i.e., price and time charts) and the inductive statistics one builds from them are simply observations without any grounding in a hypothesis. It's not that there's anything wrong with statistics per se; it is the type of statistics one uses that is the issue.

Traditional technical analysis is purely inductive reasoning that purports to observe reality, but because it lacks the most important input for any statistical model—that of the testable hypothesis—it lacks any ability to say anything concrete.

The scientific method is a form of positivist methodology, which centers on the falsification of a hypothesis or theory. If, through observation or experimentation, you can produce a predictable result that is in conflict with your hypothesis, then the hypothesis has been proven false. If you cannot produce such a result, then the hypothesis has the potential to be true and remains true until proven false.

The most famous example of this form of thinking is the *black swan* thought experiment. Our hypothesis is that, because we have never seen a black swan, *all swans are white*. The minute that we observe a black swan, our hypothesis has been falsified—that is, proven false—and we must necessarily throw it out, no matter how many times we've observed white swans. Just because we saw 100,000,000 white swans before observing a black swan does not mean that the black swan's existence can be ignored simply because it does not fit our hypothesis (or model). The single instance of a black swan cannot be outweighed by our previous 100,000,000 observations.

Technical analysis cannot produce with any certainty falsifiable hypotheses, as it is based completely on inductive reasoning. As philosopher Karl Popper concluded, no hypothesis, theory, or proposition can speak about an observation unless it is falsifiable. Ultimately, the rules of TA are more akin to observational studies that note correlations but cannot prove causality. When two things correlate with each other, it does not mean that one necessarily caused the other to happen.

In addition, the hypothesis itself must come from a deductive reasoning process, which should be based on our descriptive statistical data. Sherlock Holmes is the epitome of deductive reasoning, and it is what makes him such a seminal figure in literature. The deductive, methodical detective is something that we all strive to be in our own areas of keen interest. For me it is trading and investing. For others their passions may be inflamed by baseball, the cello, or pancreatic cancer.

Inductive reasoning without the grounding of a deductively created hypothesis lacks any anchor to the human condition, because it is just data. Data can tell you nothing in and of itself. Data without context is like a graph without units on the axes. Therefore, it is only capable of providing observations about data that are self-referential and fundamentally faulty.

Generating an investment or trading thesis is central to my view of markets; therefore, these theses need to be tested.

TA relies on our ability to recognize patterns and it is rife with the problems outlined above. Since the markets are nothing more than the behavior of everyone who is trading those commodities, a chart of price and activity (volume traded) through time paints a picture for you of what everyone thinks of the subject of that chart. The technical analyst then strives to be an expert in pattern recognition.

He is king of the ant pile built on a foundation of quicksand.

Human behavior is guided by enlightened self-interest. But people are notorious for altering their behavior when they are being observed and making decisions that to an outside observer seem to be against their best interest. This is why the scientific method (positivism) as it applies to the social sciences is an inherently flawed approach to studying behavior. And this is why, despite all of our desire, we cannot create a predictive model of the markets. Between our lack of perfect information about why we act and our range of responses to that imperfect information, the best we can do with our deductions is assign a probability of something happening.

Each person has a different set of priorities for assessing the value of an action or a thing, and we are not privy to them anymore than someone else is privy to why you decided on what to eat for dinner.

Price charts show only what people have done. They cannot tell us *why* they did what they did. A lot of financial writing seeks to discuss market movements in terms of human motivations. As there is no way of knowing *why* people do what they do, traders, necessarily, should not care about this at all if they want to be successful.

Reading Is Fundamental

As a trader, peoples' motivations are not your concern; it is not strictly true to say that peoples' motives for their actions are unknowable. You could, of course, call me up and ask me why I chose to have a steak for dinner last night and I could tell you. How that knowledge is useful to you is beyond me, but the point still stands. It is true in a practical sense. When considering the sheer magnitude of the market, though, it is irrelevant. So, it is important to ignore what we may think are the motivations of traders that compelled them to buy a stock as opposed to sell it. All we know is that they did and that will have to suffice for building any kind of trading system that has a hope of being successful. Analyzing our own motivations is hard enough; attempting to analyze the motivations of a couple thousand other people is beyond Herculean.

If *technical analysis* is ultimately a descriptive tool that can describe the past without much hope of commenting on the future, then *fundamental analysis* is the set of tools you use to consider the structural underpinnings of a market or stock. Fundamental analysis looks at how well the company is run by calculating metrics learned in MBA schools and the reasons why they are important. It also considers the macroeconomic conditions that the company is operating within, including political stability of the operating country, trends in input costs like commodities and labor, the costs of debt versus equity financing, access to public infrastructure and/or government contracts, and, most important, macroeconomic trends and local capital inflows.

Fundamental analysis is focused on research: data gathering and synthesis. It begins with asking questions, not looking at numbers. The most important question is "What information do I need?" Once armed with the right questions, you can set out to gather the information you need to reach a decision about a potential investment. If technical analysis is a snapshot of a moment in a company's history, then fundamental analysis is the company's story.

Your research may begin with an industry you believe you know something about, something related to your job or hobby. You can research a company's financial statements and note things like return on investment (ROI), net cash flow, gross profit margins, dividend yield, and so on. Any discount broker will have that information available for you. That research gives you a basic understanding of the company's ability to utilize assets and make money. It does not, however, necessarily translate into stock price appreciation due to myriad other exogenous factors, like the ones listed above.

It's important to keep in mind that the fundamental analysis you do can exist in a vacuum, disconnected from the prevailing market sentiment. No matter how good the fundamentals of a company are, if the mood of the market is bearish, then the stock will not appreciate in price; and taking a short-term position in a stock the market does not love is a waste of time and capital. It becomes an opportunity cost versus investing in another company or sector the market does love and is rewarding with investment capital.

For example, I currently work in Vietnam attempting to find value in that market. It carries with it a different set of things to focus on fundamentally than if I were looking at the U.S. or European markets. In Vietnam, capital markets are very immature and information about companies is, at best, spotty. So the data that would be at my fingertips for a country like Germany has to be dug up by hand for Vietnam. Moreover, the flow of information from the companies to the analysts (where there is one interested) is slow. Where in the West the information channel is stuffed to the point of overload, in Vietnam the channel is still being dug. It presents a challenge, but that is ultimately what business is about, overcoming challenges to fill vacuums of demand.

After that the questions get more esoteric: Is the company an industry leader or follower? Is it an Apple or an LG? Companies that are innovators are valued differently than those that ride the coattails of innovation, so a strict comparison of price/earnings growth (PEG) is not necessarily valid. For example, there is what I like to call the "Picasso premium" attached with certain companies. It's the psychological satisfaction of owning a share of a company you respect and admire, in the same way an art collector feels pride in owning work by a famous artist.

I find it interesting that fundamental analysis is changing right along with the market itself as analysts attempt to find more things to quantify to give them an edge over their competitors. I remain unconvinced that many of them can assist you in your trading, but without research there is no progress.

Inductively Coupled Failure

To make my reservations clearer, let's look at one of the newer wrinkles in research-based analysis: the data-mining strategies employed by some economists and traders today. They ask if there is a single system of rules that governs the price of all markets, across all time frames. This approach is governed by the observation of Victor Niederhoffer, who posits that markets move within "ever-changing cycles." This means that the type of trading system that worked for the equity bull market of the late 1990s may be wholly inappropriate for the bear market of 2000 to 2003.

One of the real dangers with data-mining, research-based strategies is over-fitting the model to the data and perfectly describing the past without having any ability to predict the future. Empirical data is only useful in the service of nullifying a hypothesis. And since we know that correlation does not necessarily imply causality, creating a correlative fit of past data is no guarantee of success without a sound theory based in logic and reason.

Sometimes doing an empirical fitting of the data can lead to a deduction of what the fit implies. In other words, it is possible for empirical data to reflect a truth deduced a priori, or from deductive logic.

This is not always the case, however. It is absolutely possible to hit upon an empirical fit of past data completely by accident. One of the best examples of this type of error is the story of the great physicist Niels Bohr and his solar system model of the atom. Bohr was able to create an equation that could solve for the energy of an electron in a hydrogen atom, which consists of one proton and one electron. His model matched the empirical evidence very well. His method, however, was completely wrong for any other element (i.e., those that had more than one electron). Bohr's method got the right answer for hydrogen, but for all the wrong reasons, so it was a miserable failure for all other elements. His assumptions about how the atom was structured led him to use inappropriate tools—in this case, Newtonian mechanics—to try and solve a problem governed by quantum mechanics.

Failure in the markets is simply defined by whether or not a trade is losing money. While there is a lot of discussion about analysis and research in this book, it is really aimed at traders, not analysts. Yes, you need good analytic skills to be able to make sense of the data that is coming at you. Yes, it is absolutely critical that you ask the right questions of the market and come to conclusions that grant you the insight to take a position with a high probability of exiting at a higher price.

But you also have to be willing to take money from other people. Traders have no remorse about this. They do not create value, but rather see opportunities to exploit the reassessment of value for a stock, bond, futures contract, or physical item. Moreover, at a fundamental level, you must not care that the person on the other side of the trade made or lost money. It is irrelevant.

You have to be able to look in the mirror and know whether you are the kind of person who feels no regret sitting down at a poker table and licking his lips at the thought of cleaning out a bunch of drunks who, at that moment, have more money than brains and no ability to play poker.

Are you that person? Or are you the kind of person who will spend all night trying to figure out where your edge is? Lose sleep over it?

If you find yourself acting that way about trading, then at your core you are like me. If not, however, you may be the type of person who analyzes the market, makes one or two bets based on your analysis, and rides them all the way to the bottom because, dammit, you know you're right about this and the market is wrong.

If this sounds familiar, you are not a trader; you are an analyst. A lot of this book will try to convince you to stop looking for motivations. It will also be harder for you to apply these concepts, and you will likely experience a lot more pain and failure than the trader will. The trader will see the edge, play it to the end for all it's worth, and immediately set out to make the next deal. The analyst will attempt to trade properly but will refuse to let go of the need to be right. For those with the analyst mind-set, it is imperative that you build your personal system around the idea of mechanical selling. Don't think about selling. Don't try and figure out whether it is a good idea or not to sell. You are losing money or the price has reached your target—that is all the reason you need to get out of a trade. Everything else—and I mean *everything else*—is just noise of your own devising.

If you don't heed this advice, more often than not the results will be disastrous, and failure, even if your thesis proved to be correct later on, will be reflected on your balance sheet.

The Big Trade

I chose the phrase *balance sheet* very carefully after asking some very pointed questions about your motivations for trading. As I said before, to be a trader means divorcing yourself from not only your emotions, as much as that's possible, but also from the emotions of the person on the other side of the trade. There is, however, a fine line.

Trading is a business, just like any other. Beginning traders, therefore, are entrepreneurs—and I believe very strongly in entrepreneurship. While I was studying to become a better trader, I was actually creating an illusion for myself. What I was really doing was learning how to become an entrepreneur. I was an entrepreneur whose business was trading stocks and futures, as opposed to opening a restaurant. The risks are similar; it is learning what works and what does not that is different. As the reason I wanted to write this book was so those who wanted to try their hand at being an entrepreneur would have a guide.

Every day, the Internet creates opportunities that restore the spirit of entrepreneurism back into a world where it was previously unavailable to so many people. The disruptive nature of the Internet is creating new business models, literally daily. Trading is just one of them. In less than a generation, so many old industries and business models have been rendered obsolete. This creates a plethora of opportunities for people to reinvent themselves as whatever they want to be, while it allows them to be disruptive and innovative in ways they would never have dreamed of previously.

Fundamentally, I am very bullish on people and know that, given the chance and the encouragement, they will produce astounding things. If codifying my trading style into a book can help people build their business by providing a form of income, taking greater control of how their money is invested by a professional, and maximizing their time while minimizing their risk, then how could I not do so?

While trading is a zero-sum game, at a certain level it is also entrepreneurial in that the trader seeks to adjust the pool of capital more efficiently, just as in any other business venture. Trading does not exist outside of time any more than a restaurant does. It is driven by the desire to take what is and re-imagine it into a form that someone else prefers, and when you are a trader, that *someone else* is you.

In all ventures there is risk. And trading is a high-risk and high-reward business. Seventy percent of all new businesses fail. The probabilities of your being a successful trader are similarly low, if not lower. Those who have started their own business know that, to build it, they will work harder and longer, for less pay, than they ever have in their lives—and there's a good chance it won't work.

So, is failure an option? Sure. But that should never stop you from trying.

We're Getting the Band Back Together

While the failure of Niels Bohr was ultimately a very good thing for physics and chemistry because it helped propel our understanding of atomic structure forward, it is not my goal, nor should it be yours, to be remembered for our failures. Failures are opportunities for growth and understanding, but only within the context of being successful. Failure can then be defined on a trade-by-trade basis, not a systemic failure of method.

In other words, building a marriage of high-probability setups and quantitative research methods is the broader goal. The best trading systems are those built on probabilities and distributions, not absolutes. Understanding that the best we can do is identify the tendency for a market to move in a particular direction under certain circumstances will save you a lot of emotional stress and, more importantly, a lot of money. Letting go of the idea that there is some ideal system capable of predicting the market is central to my approach to trading.

Anyone who plays Texas Hold'em should know that holding the best cards down, a pair of aces, only gives you, at best, a 60 percent chance of winning the hand. Getting dealt aces is great, but it's still not a thoughtless process to get out of a hand with your money intact. The same thing applies in the market. A stock could be in a sector with great fundamentals, have impressive earnings and cash flow, and you can even have picked a near perfect entry point for the stock given the time you decided to buy. And guess what?

You can still lose money on the trade.

That's the bad news. The good news is that I believe the merging of quantitative research and market expertise, chart analysis, and timing is not only possible but is the most successful approach to trading today.

On the one hand, a review of the most successful hedge funds reveals a preponderance of the use of *quant shops*, which are departments of mathematicians doing high-order regressions and solving sets of differential equations to create a risk model and expectation of return. In essence they are attempting to reduce the markets to a trading algorithm. Their goal in creating these algorithms is to remove human judgment from their trading, following the belief that the human making the decision is the weakest link in the system.

On the other hand, some of the most famous investors—Warren Buffet and Peter Lynch, for example—employ extensive research and due diligence in their approach, but always, in the end, rely on their personal instincts to make a decision. They take in all of the information they can and perform their own reduction of the data. Their success is proof that, while purely quantitative strategies can capture market expertise to a certain degree, it is not possible to reduce everything to an abstract regression of numbers without a human context.

Ultimately, what I am advocating is a trading system that is simple in its design. (Maybe I've learned more from Steve Jobs than I originally thought.) The iPad and iPhone stress simplicity of design, creating devices that are at once extremely attractive while also being powerful in fulfilling their intended function. As I refined my trading techniques over time, I came to appreciate this approach. As opposed to using charts filled with myriad indicators and lines defining what had happened in the past—and often sending mixed messages for my brain to process—I focus solely on the two things that matter most: price and volume.

Like a painter beginning with a blank canvas, the investor is going to include only what is needed to create the picture. This is my approach to trading, boiled down to its four basic steps:

1. Define the probability of a stock moving above/below the previous day's high/low.
2. Define the opening range for the prospective trading opportunity.
3. Measure the distribution of the size of the move.
4. Define the probability of when the move will reverse.

Understanding comes from watching the tape and seeing how price patterns emerge, and I keep only the most important statistics handy to remind me of the probability that a change in the market will take place. Through repetition of testing and observation, an instinctual trading process emerges.

Using these concepts and example exercises, I'll show you my tools for building a simple set of crib notes for a market, stock, or commodity. When I have traded like this, armed with a short list of facts about a target market and my mind free of clutter, I have produced my most consistently positive results.

Summary

- Curb your enthusiasm. The market is a treacherous place designed to part you from your money. Learn how to trade before putting any money at risk.
- Study becomes its own reward. Would you wire your house without learning about electricity?
- Technical analysis is based on a series of flawed assumptions that create poor cognitive feedback.
  - Your mind is designed to trick you into seeing patterns that can't help you trade.
  - Boiling markets down to known probabilities removes the distractions created by the pattern recognition centers of your brain.
- Fundamental analysis is essentially the search for finding value. Prediction based on modeling the past is a fool's errand.
- Traders are entrepreneurs, and how you approach risk management of your capital is the essence of your business model.
- The trading system:
  - Define your probability of success by measuring the move versus the stock's past behavior.
  - Define the probability of a reversal based on those same statistics.
  - Don't play long odds and short money.

Chapter 2

The Conditions of Change

The velocity of a body remains constant unless the body is acted upon by an external force.
—*Isaac Newton's First Law of Motion*

Livin' on the Edge

Every painting has one thing in common, regardless of subject or quality: They all start as blank pieces of canvas. It is the process of the artist pouring what is in his mind onto the canvas that creates the art. Producing that painting is intimately tied up with the artist's state of being at the time he worked on it. If he were to delay even a day, the final result would be subtly different than it would have been the day before.

As our experiences accumulate, we become different people, integrating our new experiences into our past to create who we are in the present. In hindsight, the artist will be aware of these changes in himself, while the viewer of his work will likely miss it. In fact, the viewer will impose his own experiences onto his interpretation of the painting, creating a unique perspective on the work that could not exist without both people.

This is a good metaphor for a price chart. But it is also a trap, in that the metaphor can be used from both perspectives in a multistable way that I brought up in Chapter 1. We can frame the metaphor from the perspective of the company itself, noting that the chart exists as a snapshot of the market's perception of the company's value. On the other hand, we can view it as a canvas to re-interpret in our own image, drawing various lines and bands on it to tease out meaning.

Are we accepting the chart at face value? Or are we reifying it, teasing out triangles and wedges, cups and handles, heads and shoulders?

Figure 2.1 and Table 2.1 highlight this point. Figure 2.1 is a two-year chart of Merck (MRK). I have drawn some traditional trend lines to connect highs and lows, which indicate parallel line price channels, as seen on the right side of the chart. These show what I think is important about the chart. How is this any more or less valid than someone else's interpretation? Why not use chicken entrails instead of technical analysis? Table 2.1 is simply a table of the most recent data I could find on MRK, and it tells me a lot about what they are doing as a company and what some of what they will achieve. Wouldn't you rather work from a set of numbers that you can verify and test than a set of rules and scribbles that are completely subjective?

For me, interpretations of graphs are interesting at best, but only in hindsight. They can tell you what you should have

The Conditions of Change

Figure 2.1 Traditional Technical Analysis Example

Table 2.1 Company Snapshot

Price	$38.56
Market Cap	$117.5 billion
TTM Earnings	$1.37
Dividend Yield	4.40%
TTM P/E	$28.19
Forward P/E	$10.07
PEG Ratio	$2.23
Profit Margin	8.84%
Return on Equity	7.52%

SOURCE: Yahoo! Finance

done in the past but could not tell you that at the moment they were being drawn, and hence are useless to you as a trader.

Later on, I will discuss consolidation versus trending markets, but will do so with the knowledge that even those definitions are subjective. Concepts of trend and range are the first opportunity for interpretive error. What we know is simply what has already happened. In the end there is only price: high, low, open, close, volume, and so on.

For me this is my "edge." Every trader needs to have an edge, and this one is mine.

In a world of hyper-information, stripping out the noise and focusing on a small set of probabilities and trading setups is the only path to consistent success in trading. This is what will allow you to note outlying information and use it to make quick, accurate, and remorseless decisions. It is about simplicity of design, maximizing the effects of the tools you use, and distilling those tools down to convey as much relevant information as they can without sowing confusion.

In considering the tension between complexity of function and simplicity of design, Yahoo CEO Marissa Mayer said this while she worked at Google: "Google has the functionality of a really complicated Swiss Army knife, but the home page is our way of approaching it closed. It's simple, it's elegant. You can slip it into your pocket, but it's got the great doodad when you need it. A lot of our competitors are like a Swiss Army knife open—and that can be intimidating and occasionally harmful."[1]

In other words, there is a reason we no longer use the command line to run our computers.

I want my trading tools to be like a closed Swiss Army Knife—available to help me with the right information at the right time and then be put away until the next time I need them.

Simplicity for its own sake is no goal either. Done poorly, simplification will remove information that is vital. The goal when simplifying is to subtract the obvious and add meaning. In poetry, words are at a premium. The goal of the poet is to use as few words as possible to convey maximum meaning. Haiku demands you say something meaningful about your emotional state in exactly seventeen syllables. Why not have trading tools that are like haiku?

I am forever trying to simplify my trading tools so that the ones that remain are vested with the most information and

---

[1] "Simple. The Next Killer App," SustainableWork, Web, 11/6/2005, http://blog.sustainablework.com/2005/11/simplethe-killer-app.html

the least amount of personal interpretation. This is why I have no time or use for traditional forms of technical analysis. I feel they needlessly complicate the story that price and volume already tell and, left to their own devices, will eventually consume a person's every thought, destroying his ability to make sound decisions.

The analogies of trading to poker are obvious and instructive but, since the theme of this book is simplicity, there is an even better one to use—that of a game of hot potato. He who holds the potato at the end is the loser. In the market at the end of a rally, the person who bought the stock last is the loser. He has purchased at a price that will most likely reverse, leaving him having overpaid for the stock.

Your edge is in knowing when to cash out and pass the potato on before the music stops playing.

Refining your timing will allow you to eke out incrementally higher gains per trade. This is what I meant earlier about failure within the context of succeeding. You may have failed to earn as big a profit on a trade as you could have, but you still earned a profit. Don't beat yourself up for what you didn't achieve; failure is gestated with negative thinking. Congratulate yourself on what you accomplished and look for opportunities for improvement next time.

Failure is gestated with negative thinking.

Everyone in the market needs an edge. The purpose of the next few sections will be to define the basic framework for developing a method to trading. I will demonstrate to you how it works. After that it comes down to repetition and experience, until you become the best trader you are capable of being.

Closing Time

In order to build any edge, however, you will have to learn the significance of price action. During any given period of time there are four prices that are measurable, which means that we tend to gravitate toward them in our analysis. We are data junkies, after all. Our brains are fantastic processing machines whose primary function is to take in stimuli, attach meaning to them, and eventually make decisions based on our findings.

The four prices that matter are the *high*, the *low*, the *open*, and the *close*. They are pretty straightforward in their definitions: The high is the highest price transacted during the bar, while the low is the lowest. The open can be thought of as the first price at which a transaction took place, while the close is the price of the last trade during the time period. Examples of each can be seen in Table 2.2.

That said, however, each price—open, close, high, and low—signifies something different. We'll take them individually and explain what's happening at each of them. While all of these concepts are applicable for any time frame, there are certain conditions that happen only at the beginning and end of each trading session. So, with that in mind, for the purposes of discussion, a bar or candle will represent a day.

The candlestick is a simple tool for visualizing the four prices that have been around for thousands of years. Figure 2.2

Table 2.2 Historical Weekly Data Example

Date	Open	High	Low	Close
4/9	1397.45	1397.45	1357.38	1368.71
4/2	1408.47	1422.38	1392.92	1398.08
3/26	1397.11	1419.15	1391.56	1408.47
3/19	1404.17	1414.00	1386.87	1397.11
3/12	1370.78	1405.88	1366.69	1404.17
3/5	1369.59	1374.76	1340.03	1370.87
2/27	1365.20	1378.04	1354.92	1369.63
2/21	1361.22	1368.92	1352.28	1365.74
2/13	1343.06	1363.4	1340.80	1361.23
2/6	1344.32	1354.32	1335.92	1342.64
1/30	1316.16	1345.34	1300.49	1344.90
1/23	1315.29	1333.47	1306.06	1316.33
1/17	1290.22	1315.49	1290.22	1315.38
1/9	1277.83	1296.82	1274.55	1289.09
1/3	1258.86	1284.62	1258.86	1277.81

The Conditions of Change 33

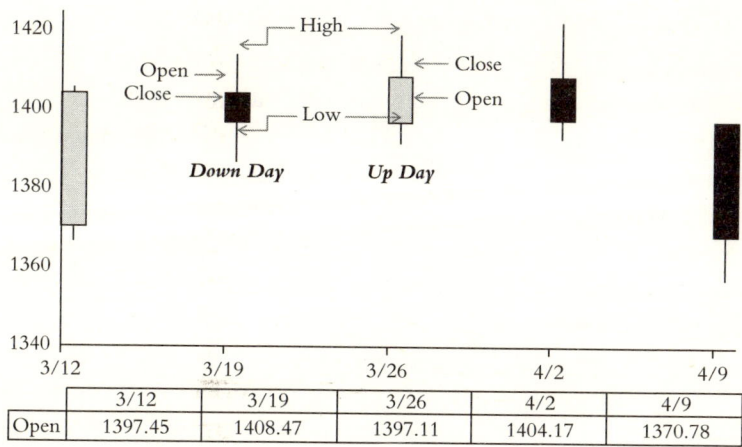

Figure 2.2 Candlestick Chart of Open, High, Low, Close

has a breakdown of the two types of candlesticks. Like all good tools, they are feature rich and easy to use.

Like with any good story, it makes sense to start at the beginning, which means the *opening price*. Built into the opening price is all of the new information the market has tried to absorb since the previous day's close. This can be as dramatic as a missed earnings report or U.S. unemployment data, and as inconsequential as Estonian GDP capacity utilization figures. What is important to remember about the open is that it is an unsettled price, a best guess by the market makers as to where the stock or index should be trading relative to what is happening in the futures market and other factors.

Contained within the open is a lot of pent-up energy, both bullish and bearish, that has to be resolved and will be during the initial minutes of trading. It is at the open that transactions are dominated by retail investors who have put in standing orders with their brokers before heading off to work and amateur daytraders who get caught up in the excitement and adrenaline of those crazy opening moments of trading.

If the opening price is lower than the previous day's close that puts the market in a bearish posture that will have to be worked through during the session. The converse of this is true as well: A market that starts higher than the previous day's close is full of bullish energy and does not start trading at sale prices.

Saying this, however, does not preclude the bears overtaking the bulls and driving the price lower during the day. It just means that at the open the mood is bullish or bearish relative to yesterday's closing price. It is important to remember it is the job of financial media to treat all economic data as significant and make you believe that whatever it is they are talking about is of the utmost importance—after all, their revenue comes from ratings and page views.

Your job as the trader is to cut through that noise, care about price first, and listen to the market. The noise from the pre-market chatter is just as distracting as any trend line or moving average line.

The *high* and the *low* are mirror images of each other and define the day's range. Both of them can very often be set during the first 15 to 30 minutes of trading. Whatever high price is established during the opening shake-out period is the first hurdle for any potential intraday move higher. High prices from previous days also act as barriers (resistance), as they represent price levels previous bulls were unable to maintain. So they naturally become places where bears will lie in wait and test the current bulls' commitment to bidding prices higher.

The low price is the opposite of the high price, and all of the same conditions that apply to the high price apply to the low. The difference, of course, is that the roles are reversed. If bears want to take the price lower, they will have to push through the intraday low and possibly some previous low prices to do so. These interim low prices become support for prices, places where bulls lie in wait to absorb selling from the bears, accumulating stock and exhausting the bears temporarily.

Both the low and the high may be violated many times during the day, and because of this, they do not have particular significance or power to act as support or resistance. They are, however, the initial magnets that traders will test to uncover potential opposition.

But all of these moves mean very little in comparison to the *close* or *closing* price. Another way to look at the closing price is that it is the level at which current holders are comfortable with the risk of owning the stock until trading resumes. For many, that involves the risk of holding the stock while being on margin. In the words of Peter Brandt, the close is the "put up or shut up" price. It is subject to all of the things that create the pent-up energy that has to be dealt with the next day and that will define whether your position is strengthened or weakened.

If the open is dominated by retail investors, the close or, more specifically, the period just before the close is dominated by institutional investors. They have little to no margin risk associated with their position and will gladly sit back and let retailers, the day-traders, and the HFT algorithms duke it out until they begin squaring their positions (i.e., selling out and getting into cash) before making their next moves.

The closing price is indicative of strong-handed price action. These institutional buyers are working on much longer time frames than a day or a week. They are looking to scale into a position, buying small tranches of stock over a period of time to establish an average buying price as they amass a large position without moving the price substantially.

They will also use the high volume generated by the day traders' settling up to buy and sell into it without greatly affecting price. The net effect is that the direction of the close relative to the rest of the day's trading is indicative of what the institutional money is doing, on balance buying or selling. If the price rises into the close they are buying and vice versa.

The margin risk associated with holding a position overnight is the reason why the final close for the week, normally Friday, is of particular importance. Not only is it the closing price for the day, but it's also the close for the week, so all of the risk associated with holding overnight is multiplied exponentially by holding over the weekend.

This also means that significant trading events—for example, besting a particularly strong area of resistance or support—that happen on the close of trading on a Friday carry a lot more weight than the same thing happening on a Wednesday.

On June 15, 2012, the S&P 500 saw a lot of volume transacted, more than five times the amount normally traded, during the last 30 minutes of trading and just after the close in the futures markets. That was the last trading session before the Greek elections that may have created havoc in the markets come Monday morning. But with all of that buying, the "smart money" was on stability as the Greek people voted to maintain E.U. membership and continued access to the euro as their currency.

It turned out that the bullish investors were correct in their take on the situation in Greece, as the election came out the way the equity markets wanted and the S&P 500 opened near that bullish close at 1342.42 and closed up slightly at 1344.78. While the Greek election had the market in a bullish mood, the Spanish bond market did not and sapped any enthusiasm the bulls had that day. That June 15 closing price was the highest close since May 11, 2012, the Friday after the initial Greek election, which spooked the markets. But, going into that weekend long or short anything was riskier than normal, even though institutions were bullish.

The Outsiders

The first edge you will need in your quest for trading success is knowing about one of the most consistently true behaviors that the market exhibits that has nothing to do with fundamentals or trends or when the music will stop.

Inside Day

One in which the price range for the current day is completely circumscribed by the previous day's range.

The Conditions of Change

I mentioned in Chapter 1 that one of the core principles in my trading system is defining the probabilities of a stock surpassing the previous day's high or low by assessing the distribution of those occurrences. In my research to put a framework to this principle, I came across this statistic in the trading activity of the S&P 500 Index: Since 1999, over 3,248 trading days, there have been just 395 that could be defined by the term inside day. It turns out that over the past century this behavior is consistent; seven out of every eight days, the S&P 500 will violate the previous day's high or low, and sometimes both. This is a very significant observation. Another conclusion teased from the statistics is that as activity (volume) on the exchanges increases, so does the volatility.

I would encourage you to analyze any stock you think may be worth your investment. Go ahead and grab three to five years' worth of data (daily high, low, open, close, and volume) and copy it into a spreadsheet. Then, using a conditional function (i.e., an If/then function; see Tip sidebar for Excel grammar), you can find out how often the high or low from the previous day will be tested. (See Table 2.3 for details.) A value of 1 in the "High/Low Tested?" column means the previous day's high or low was breached.

Tip

Function to Use in Excel

=IF(High#2>High#1), 1, 0)

or =IF(Low#2<Low#1), 1, 0)

Once you have done this, sum up the "High/Low Tested?" column and divide that result by the total number of observations. You now have the probability of the breadth of an intraday move heading toward the previous extreme. Table 2.3 is a simple

Table 2.3 Example of High/Low Back-Testing

Sample #	High	Low	Close	Volume	High/Low Tested?
1	$371.15	$363.32	$363.57	909800	1
2	$375.84	$366.88	$366.99	15295400	1
3	$374.55	$370.94	$376.51	14607900	0
4	$371.68	$365.91	$369.01	15999300	1
5	$379.99	$374.88	$374.94	13283500	1
Total					4/5 or 80%

example with only five observations. The larger the data set you use for this type of quantitative analysis, the more statistically valid it will be. One doesn't have to have an extensive background in statistics to do this; it's just simple arithmetic. For a three-year subset of the data presented above (2008 to 2011), the probability of the high being breached was 45.6 percent and the low, 54.5 percent. The average range of prices for any one day was 1.77 points. Less than 10 percent of days were inside days.

As the price approaches the previous day's high or low, we are presented with a trading opportunity because we know that the odds are in our favor that level will be breached. Since the beginning of the current wave of financial stress, over 90 percent of days do exactly that. As I said before, this edge is one of the most reliable edges in trading, and it bears emphasizing. In nine days out of ten there is an opportunity to scalp a portion of the day's price action simply because the buyers and sellers will attempt to probe outside of the previous day's price range. We will get into the mechanics of how to place the trade once the price creates the outside day condition in the next few sections.

Living Day to Day

Now, let's go through an example of how to create a quantitative tool to aid you in your trading activities. A number of the tools I've built have come out of simply observing the market and seeing something that I think is interesting. It does no good, however, to have an observation without doing a little bit of work to figure out if the observation is significant or just a form of confirmation bias, seeing what you want to see and then making decisions based on it. Remember the multistable images in Chapter 1? Your brain searches these observations out and is inherently lazy, so you have to go back and use something that is observationally neutral—mathematics—to verify its significance.

Let's take an easy example that is both borne out of observation and backed up by what we would expect of the markets, and I'll develop it into a tool. We're going to take a look at the effect of the day of the week on the behavior of the market. In essence, we are asking the question "Does the market trade differently on Monday as opposed to any other day of the week?"

We would assume this to be true since, by the time the market opens on Monday morning, the world has had nearly three days to change and create new information that traders and investors will feel compelled to act on. In addition to this wealth of information, there is also an effect from people playing catch-up on the events of the past week. Not everyone who is in the markets eats, breathes, and follows everything during the week. Even with the advent of smartphones, near-instantaneous information, 24-hour cable, and internet financial news feeds, a large number of market participants are frankly busy going about their business, engaging in the very activities that the market is reacting to. If everyone was watching the market, there wouldn't be any real work getting done, now would there?

Therefore, it is reasonable to assume that a great percentage of both retail and even institutional investors are spending a portion of their weekend reviewing the week's activity and formulating an action plan for the upcoming week.

And we would be correct. Monday is the most extreme day of the week. Figure 2.3 is a chart of more than five years' worth of trading on the S&P 500, going back to the beginning of 2007. Thirty-two percent of all Mondays set the low for

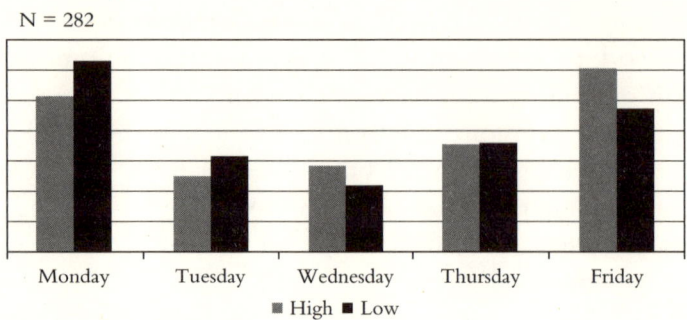

Figure 2.3 Effect of Day of the Week on Market Behavior (S&P 500 2007 to June 2012)
SOURCE: Yahoo! Finance

the week, while 26 percent set the high for the week. Of the 282 weeks in this data set, Monday set either the week's low or high in 159 weeks, or 56.3 percent. Only two Mondays since 2007 have set both the low and the high for the week, so when Monday is bearish it gives you a very good place to set a stop for any trade you plan to pull off during that week.

Looking more closely at Figure 2.3, it is obvious that Friday and Monday are reversed in their frequency of setting the high and the low for the week. This actually brings up a great follow up question to our original one:

If Monday is the low or high for the week, on which day is the opposite condition most likely to occur?

Figure 2.4 has our answer. It is a chart of the distribution of the frequency of highs and lows for each day of the week, following a high or low on the Monday of that week. The gray series represents the day on which the market made the high for the week after making the low for the week on Monday. The black series is exactly the opposite, the distribution of the weekly lows made after the weekly high was made on Monday.

Emphatically, Friday is the most likely day on which to see the opposite of what happened on Monday. Forty-nine percent of the time when the low for the week was made on Monday, the high for the week was made on Friday, as shown in the gray bar.

The Conditions of Change

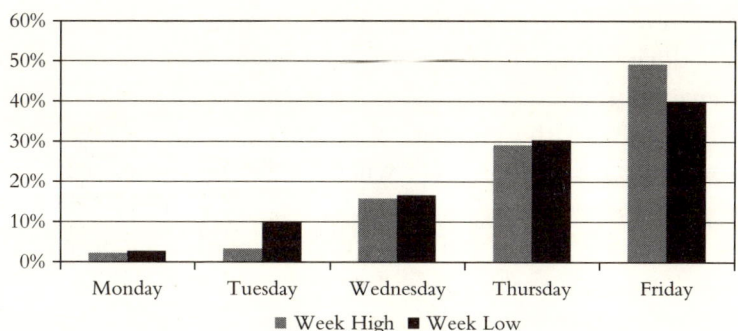

Figure 2.4 Monday High/Low Distribution of the Opposite Condition
Source: Yahoo! Finance

This simple look at the market, which was based on a pretty safe deduction about human behavior, not only yields data that confirms our hypothesis but also gives us a basis to guide us in our decision making within a known probability of success.

We now know that if we buy near the low on a Monday when the market is bearish, a state most likely to produce the low for the week, that we stand a very good chance (78 percent) of being able to sell at the highest price for the week on either Thursday or Friday. Setting a stop at the low for Monday protects your capital.

For investors with a longer focus, it gives us an action plan as to when during a week we should open our position. If the market is in a bearish mood on a Monday, then we can buy with greater confidence, having picked a low entry point for our position.

Even more powerful is the opposite situation. One in three Mondays set the high for the week, and half of the Fridays following a high Monday, set the low for the week. Waiting to buy a stock until Thursday or Friday after a strong Monday market gives you a great chance to pay a lower price for the stock than you would have on Monday.

The reason for this behavior is that extremes in sentiment are often overstated in the markets and need to be corrected. Market-moving information from the weekend will produce an extreme reaction when the market opens on Monday, but then during the week, the natural tendency is for people to believe in stability not catastrophe. Moreover, not everyone will agree with the popular sentiment or react to it with the same agenda; therefore, there will be a natural move away from the extreme position. The cyclical nature of intraweek trading is just one example of how you can refine your probability of making a profitable trade. I've done this for the S&P 500 to illustrate how the broad market trades. After I first got to Vietnam, I did a similar analysis on the VN Index and observed the same pattern of Monday and Friday behavior, even though the structure of the Vietnamese market is completely different. Individual stocks will trade differently, of course, and I recommend you do this kind of analysis on any stock you plan on trading and incorporate it into your plan.

Sold to the Highest Bidder

The regularity with which the market violates its previous high or low provides a backdrop for the price movements we are likely to see day to day. I think it's instructive to now step back a bit and remind ourselves what it is that we are actually doing when we trade.

It's easy to lose sight that the market is just people buying and selling stuff. It is a giant auction where everything is for sale and the highest bidder wins. All markets operate on the same principle: supply versus demand. In the end, if the supply of buyers outstrips the supply of sellers at a particular price then the price must rise to balance out the supply of the commodity.

But saying it that way misses the point because a rising price is a *consequence* of bidders in the market; it is not the *driver*. In an auction-style market, sellers post their wares for sale at their desired price, while buyers state the limit they are willing to pay. It is only when there are buyers and sellers who agree on a price that a transaction is made.

Auction market theory (AMT) combines price with volume in its analysis to arrive at what is called the *market condition*. This is simply the state of the market with respect to the number of buyers and sellers around a fair-value price. The goal is to arrive at an understanding of what kind of market we are in and the probability that the market will shift from one state to another.

In AMT there are only two market states: *consolidation* and *trending*. A market is consolidating if it is trading in a range around a fair market value. If the market has determined that, in light of new information, the range of the near past is inadequate to satisfy buyers and sellers, then it will leave the current range and trend toward a new one, up or down. The financial markets vacillate between these two states endlessly, first consolidating and then trending until a new level is found to trade around, *ad nauseum, ad infinitum*. For as long as there are humans walking this planet, this oscillation of price and volume will continue.

Because of this constant oscillation, the classic price-and-time chart, while helpful, is not the limit of our potential knowledge of what is actually happening during a trading session. The price-and-time chart is capable of showing us the four big prices (open, high, low, close) and the total volume, but not how much of that volume was transacted under the following conditions:

1. At a particular price within the time represented by the bar.
2. Whether it was traded at the bid price versus the asking price.
3. At the price where the most trading occurred.

Before I go any further, I should probably quickly go over the bid price and the asking price. These are fairly straightforward. On one side, we have the bid price, which is simply the price being offered by a potential buyer. He's putting up an order that says, "I'm willing to buy up to 1,000 shares of XYZ Corp. for no more than $1.10 per share." His bid would be $1.10, just like in a physical auction.

On the other side, we have the asking price, which is the exact opposite. It is the price that a potential seller wishes to sell his stock for, in essence saying, "I'm willing to sell my 1,000 shares of XYZ Corp. for $1.12." In this case, $1.12 would be the asking price and $0.02 would be the spread; the difference between the bid and the ask.

With this in mind, you can now sit and watch the ticker and see how the market unfolds in real time, assessing how the interplay of the supply of buyers and sellers changes with time. By putting up a chart and a price ticker that shows you the bid and ask prices as well as the size of the volume on each side, you can begin to get a feel for the rhythm of the market you are watching.

Going one step further you can put up a *time and sales* feed, which will show you, in real time, what trades have occurred. This type of feed will tell you how many shares were traded, at what price, and whether or not the price was at the bid, the ask, or in between. If you watch one of these long enough you will see trades happen outside of the bid and the ask; there are any number of reasons why that would happen, but nearly all trades—more than 99.9 percent—happen between the bid and the ask.

I don't recommend trading with real money at first. Instead, use a virtual trading account, like those available either through your broker or a site like Yahoo! Finance. Set up an account and trade virtual shares for points. Think of it as a game with a goal to reach, and do this for a while. Don't jump right into trading with real money after a few days; trading today is much more complicated than it was in years past due to the advent of *high frequency trading* systems and cross-linked exchanges. The principles are the same, but the behavior is different. We will get into why and how later in the book.

As you practice to understand how orders, both to buy and sell, enter and flow through a market, you can move from being a novice looking to find predictability in a market toward being a professional who understands that there is no prediction, only probability—and that probability has to be continually reassessed as time goes on. During these early sessions you can begin to create rules for yourself about how big a position to take, how long to hold it, and so on.

Moreover, you can get a sense of the energy of the market and how activity comes in waves, sometimes building slowly after a long period of nearly no action, and other times coming on in a torrent, almost too quickly for you to react to. But this is not the dominant behavior in the market.

Most of the time markets are consolidating in a range of prices. Sometimes that range is very broad and sometimes it is very narrow, depending on the time frame under scrutiny and the conditions the market is operating within. In addition, not only is consolidation the dominant state in terms of time spent, it is also where most of the volume occurs. To be statistically normal, a market transacts 68 percent of its volume within one standard deviation of the fair market price, the mean of the range. The other 32 percent of the volume occurs during trending moves toward the new consolidation range.

The mean of the range is very important to me. I believe in breaking down the action within a bar by establishing the mean price of the range and looking at how much volume has traded above and below that price. That gives a great indication of the current market sentiment, either bullish or bearish. If more volume is happening above the mean of the range, then that means there are more buyers than sellers in the market and the mean price is more likely to rise than fall, and vice versa.

For trading purposes, then, most of the volume traded is unimportant. It is noise, gyrating around, waiting for a change in perception to occur. When that change happens—such as through the release of a piece of news—a group of fresh buyers or sellers will come into the market. In the case of a bearish reaction, sellers will *hit the bid*, selling at the bid price out of fear. In the short term, the relative volume is extremely large, overwhelming the current number of bids taking the price lower. As the price moves down, the selling will continue until a price is reached where the supply of buyers is sufficient to soak up the selling and arrest the market's fear.

In the case of a bullish reaction, fresh buyers do the same thing. The process is known as *lifting offers*. When buyers overwhelm the current offers, sellers will pull their offers from the table in the hope of getting the buyers to pay a higher price. The move will exhaust itself once the sellers emerge *en masse* to absorb the buying and satisfy their greed.

To illustrate this, I've pulled a sample set of data from recent action on the S&P 500 (NYSE: SPY). Tables 2.4 and 2.5 show an example of the volume breakdown of a consolidation period (Table 2.4) versus a trending period (Table 2.5). Looking first at the consolidation period in Table 2.4, the average opening and closing prices were nearly identical, indicating that 116.1 was close to *fair value*. The average range was 7.9 points, which sets up a consolidation range of 112 to 120. Note that the average volume during this period was over 300 million shares traded per day.

Table 2.4 AMT Analysis of SPY Data during a Consolidation in 2011

Date	Open	High	Low	Close	Vol (mil)	Range
15-Aug	119.19	121.2	112.5	112.64	346.469	8.7
22-Aug	115.17	119.4	112.41	117.97	295.992	6.99
29-Aug	119.56	123.51	117.43	117.85	248.844	6.08
6-Sept	114.39	120.94	114.38	115.92	281.424	6.56
12-Sept	114.47	121.97	114.05	121.52	301.801	7.92
19-Sept	119.53	121.99	111.3	113.54	319.571	10.69
26-Sept	114.61	119.56	112.98	113.15	289.125	6.58
3-Oct	112.49	117.25	107.43	115.71	335.776	9.82
Mean	**116.2**	**120.7**	**112.8**	**116.0**	**302.375**	**7.9**
Std Dev.	**2.8**	**1.9**	**2.8**	**3.0**	**31.343**	**1.7**

Table 2.5 AMT Volume Analysis of SPY

Date	Open	High	Low	Close	Vol (mil)	Range
10-Oct	117.68	122.6	117.67	122.57	228.971	4.93
17-Oct	121.99	124.12	119.2	123.97	257.769	4.92
24-Oct	124.17	129.42	122.21	128.6	275.998	7.21

Volume Breakdown		
Consolidation	2,419,002,200	76.03%
Trending	762,738,800	23.97%
Total	3,181,741,000	

The Conditions of Change

Moving on to Table 2.5, we see that the price pushed through 120 during the week of October 10, 2011, despite much lower volume. That began a three-week trending move to the next range, with 128 being the high and 120 being the low (data not shown).

The takeaway here is that after a two-month consolidation where 2.4 billion shares traded could not move the market, it took 24 percent of that to lift the market higher. Moreover, if we were to go inside those numbers more closely, we would likely see that most of that volume was intraday consolidation and that the volume needed to lift offers was only a small percentage of each day. It is not the aggregate volume that matters, though that can be useful; it is the volume that hits bids or lifts offers that moves markets.

There are a number of software packages out there that compile the volume exchanged on the bidding and asking price of a stock and calculate the difference. The data is expressed as either a positive or negative number, informing you of who has the upper hand currently, the buyers or the sellers. It is these volume deltas that give you a clear direction of the flow of orders into the market with the net buy and sell volume shown at each price. This type of data flow is of immeasurable help timing entry and exit points in a trade.

Getting this data without subscribing to a data service or buying proprietary trading software is difficult. Most online or discount brokers offer you time and sales data along with charting capabilities, but they are not integrated in any meaningful way. So, again, I go back to my suggestion of watching the markets and sinking into the experience of it, watching how the orders flow and what bars are drawn based on that information.

Some people find real value in what is known as level 2 quoting, which is usually a premium service offered by a broker. Level 2 quoting doesn't just show you the volume at the bid and ask, but rather the array of the bids and asks through the entire price spectrum.

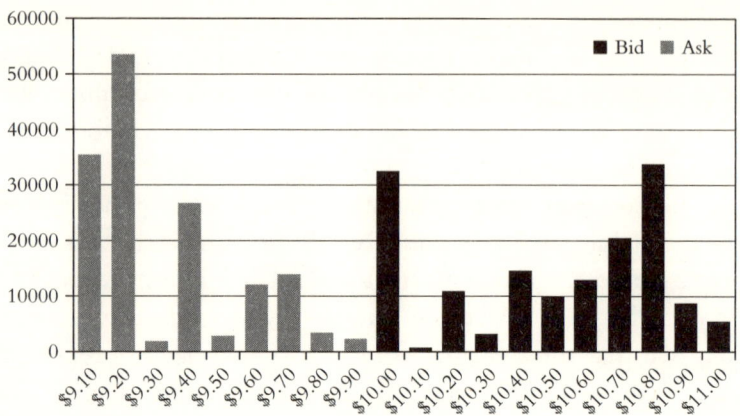

Figure 2.5 Level 2 Quote Example

In Figure 2.5, the price of the stock is trading between $9.90 and $10.00 per share. There is a lot of supply sitting on $10.00 and not a lot of demand at $9.90 or $9.80. So if sellers were to come into the market and start hitting bids, there is a high probability that they would be able to take the price down near $9.70 without much trouble. For the bulls to gain the upper hand and move the price above $10.00, they would have to buy more than five times that amount of stock than it would take for sellers to move the price below $9.80.

So, if within a given time period you are seeing volume deltas that are big relative to the size of the public bid/ask structure, then this increases the likelihood that there will be a move above or below a certain level of resistance or support.

Level 2 quoting was much more valuable information even just five or six years ago, but today so-called *dark pools* route a great deal of the supply and are not evident on a level 2 quote board because their orders exist in a conditional state held with the market maker to intentionally hide their presence.

For this reason and many others, markets are now even less predictable. It is important to simply read the current state of the market and react to it without trying to outguess it—that is a fool's errand. As we discussed earlier, technical analysis of price action often does not take into consideration the interplay of what's occurring within volume bars. AMT addresses that and provides an understanding of how the market actually functions.

Breaking It Down

Designating consolidation versus trending market states implies the same things as more traditional forms of support and resistance, which exist in all forms of technical analysis. The difference is that AMT refuses to consider that the future is predictable. It is not looking for predictive models. Rather, it is interested in assessing and continually reassessing in real time the state of the market and the probability that support or resistance will arise in a particular zone of prices. The difference is subtle, but that subtlety is a key part of the edge that this method has over traditional technical analysis.

Traders take their cues from these zones. One of the most maddening things for novices about watching the market is waiting for the price to move to where *they* think it wants to go. Psychologically, they are attempting to control the market as opposed to listening to it. They may engage in very complex or subtle forms of reification and not even realize it.

The fundamentals are all in place, they feel, yet sometimes for hours or even days there is almost no movement in price, and traders refuse to commit to one side of the trade or the other. With markets being the minefields that they are, savvy traders would rather follow an existing trend than be the trendsetters themselves. This is one of the reasons behind this market behavior. Everyone wants to be on the bus, and no one wants to be left standing on the sidewalk, or worse, run into the pavement. But if you attempt to force the market into your personal vision of what you think should happen, nothing will throw you in the bus's path faster.

There are a number of ways to identify breakouts or breakdowns from resistance or support, respectively, but no matter the method, the result is always the same: Fresh volume will enter the market quickly and the previously moribund stock price will begin to move rapidly away from the support/resistance level at the edges of the consolidation range. Volume delta is extremely useful during these initial moments when energy is building up in the price and volume. Sometimes it happens with one larger-than-normal block going by the board.

Suppose a stock has been trading in small, 100- to 300-share blocks back and forth over a few pennies for hours and the amount of volume sitting on the bid and the ask does not seem to appreciably change. Then someone finally buys up most of the supply at that price in a big trade and the market begins to react. It's like the anticipation before the beginning of a horserace or the cadence the quarterback calls out just before the snap in a football game. Once that inciting incident (to borrow a phrase from screenwriting) occurs, then all other actions are possible and a flood of responses takes place. The time leading up to a breakout is the time when the market can tell you the most—if you are listening.

This leads me to a concept called the *opening range*. The concept has been around for a long time and its definition is the first slice of the day. For day traders it is generally the first five to thirty minutes of a session, but this concept can be expanded to Monday if we are looking at a week of sessions, which calls back to our discussion of the effects of the days of the week earlier in the chapter. The high and low of that period of time is defined as the opening range. AMT would say that the market is consolidating around a fair market value within a range of prices.

The opening range can then be more broadly defined as a consolidating market condition from AMT.

The opening range allows you to create a level from which you can time your entry into the market either long or short. The opening range is the area where the majority of the trading volume will occur but without any significant effect on the price. With apologies to Shakespeare, it is a time of "sound and fury signifying nothing." If the market is behaving normally

The Conditions of Change

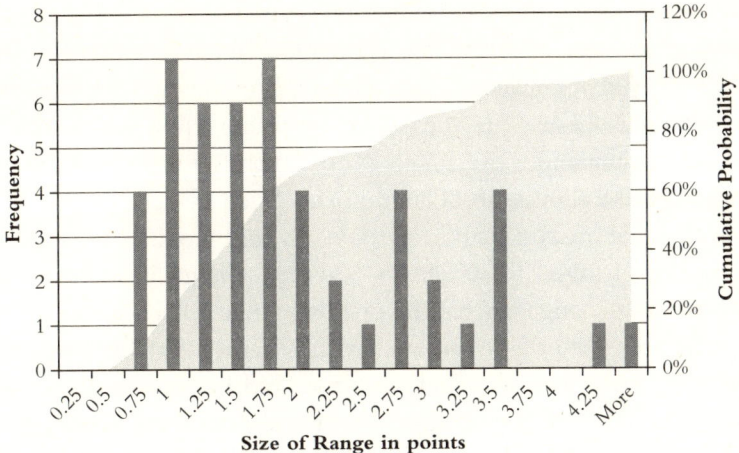

Figure 2.6 Distribution Histogram of Weekly Opening Ranges for SPY in 2011

with a Gaussian distribution of price and volume, then 68 percent of the volume will occur within the opening range.

Let us define Monday as the opening range for a week's trading. Presented in Figure 2.6 is the distribution of the price range for every Monday in 2011 through mid-November for the S&P 500 (NYSE:SPY). This is an historical document for the market, detailing both the size and the frequency of the price action on any given Monday. We can use this tool to compare the current price action with what has gone on previously to get a better idea of whether the market is consolidating, trending, or impending to breakout or reverse.

The mean of this distribution is 1.92 points, meaning that on an average Monday the difference between the high and the low for SPY would be $1.92. In the four weeks after this data set was compiled, the Monday price ranges were 1.7, 1.36, 1.74, and 1.81. Prices were tightening, which means that you can expect smaller moves before reversals and should lower your expectations per trade.

Identifying and defining the opening range is central to my style of trading. It is one of the core principles I outlined earlier.

By doing so, we are able to minimize the noise that exists in a market and get closer to answering the question "What is the probability that the next bar will go up or down?" Money can only be reliably made in the market by taking advantage of movement; consolidations are much more difficult and less reliable to trade. It is the alleviation of a temporary price arbitrage versus perceived value among market participants that provides the energy for price changes. Identifying when that energy is sufficient to achieve that change is what the opening range will do for us.

In other words, consider that the market is trading around price X, but a majority believes it should be trading at X plus fifty cents. The difference between these prices, the arbitrage—in this case fifty cents—is the opportunity to make money. All economic activity centers on this perceived mismatch in value. If everyone valued everything equally, then no one would trade anything. The equity markets are no different; they just involve so many people that their movements can feel opaque because of all of the disparate agendas that individuals bring to their perception of value.

The opening range in conjunction with the previous day's close gives me a stance to take towards the market, bullish or bearish. Figure 2.7 shows a classic opening range in action, and we'll look at it as an example of how opening range trading can be done. The first 30 minutes of the market is outlined and shows us the noise levels. The *high* of the opening range is our first potential resistance point to the upside while the *low* of the opening range is our first potential level of support to the downside. Each candlestick represents five minutes. The previous day's closing price was contained in the opening range (extreme left side of the chart), which gives us no signal of an extremely bullish or bearish attitude.

Figure 2.7 charts a stock that bounced within the opening range for another twenty minutes and then promptly sold off, breaching both the low of the opening range and the previous day's low. Based on classic opening range strategy, a small short

The Conditions of Change 53

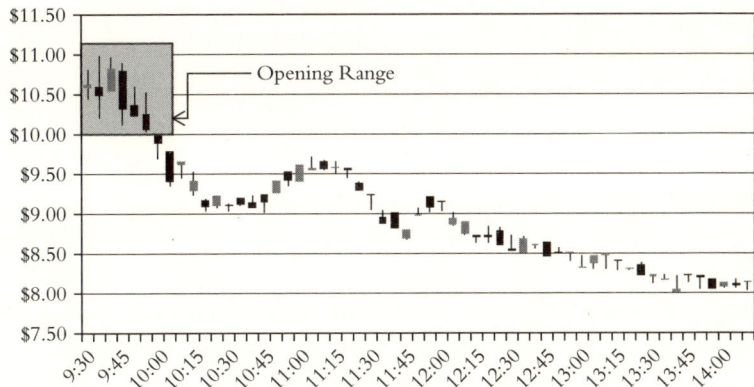

Figure 2.7 Opening Range of the First 30 Minutes of the Day

position on the drop below the low of the opening range is warranted and then covered later in the day.

Note also that in the last fifteen minutes of trading, the price dropped, indicating that institutional investors, who dominate the close of each day, were selling.

While this example is focused on an ultra-short time period, it is just as applicable to a longer time frame. Figure 2.8 is a chart of the price of Apple (AAPL) from late 2003 to late 2005. The opening range is the month of January. The closing price for 2003 was $21.37 per share.

AAPL opened the year at $21.55 per share. The opening range, defined by the trading in the month of January, was $21.28 to $24.84 per share. One can use the opening month of the year as an opening range just as we can use Monday as the opening range for the week, or the first 30 minutes as the opening range for the day. There is pent-up energy in the market based on calendar effects. For the month of January, new positions are established because it is the start of a new tax year and that affects people's behavior.

Establishing that as the opening range would have me in a bullish posture because the opening range was above the previous month's high. Since the opening range is a month

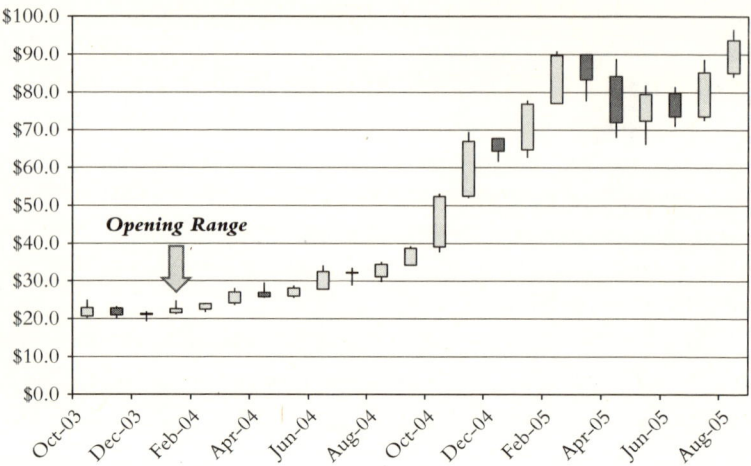

Figure 2.8 Opening Range as a Single Bar Example (AAPL Monthly Chart 2003–2005)

long, we look at the previous bar and note our stance in relation to that.

That said, I would not take a position in AAPL until the opening range was violated in some way, either up or down. During all of February, the stock meandered within the opening range. On March 4, 2004, AAPL broke through the top of the opening range on 2.5 times the average volume for January and February, and closed at $25.16. The next day it exploded upwards on 5.5 times the average volume closing at $26.74 per share. These are huge volume deltas. That was the start of a historic bull run in AAPL, which culminated in a high price of approximately $200 per share in December of 2007.

Another thing that this example highlights is that the opening range can be thought of as a single bar. We will build on this as we redefine the concept of the opening range into a more nuanced form.

Not all stocks perform like AAPL and not all trades are 900 percent winners, but the opening range is a powerful tool for refining your timing on when to enter a trade, regardless of whether you make 1 percent or 100 percent on it.

Finites Move in Infinite Markets

We're now armed with our opening ranges to guide our timing, and we know that most days are likely to breach either the previous day's high or low around 85 percent of the time, 90 percent in especially volatile markets. It is now time to consider how big the move will be, which can then define how much, if any, profit is available. The size of the breach is dependent on volume, which as we have seen has a large effect on any trending move's magnitude.

To assess how far the move could be from the opening price itself, it would make sense to see what has happened with the stock in the past. Figure 2.9 is a graph of data from the past three years of trading activity for the SPDR S&P 500 ETF (SPY). The bars represent the percentage of days where the high price exceeded the opening price and by how much. The mean of this distribution is 0.84, which means 50 percent of the time after moving that far from the opening price SPY has stopped rising. The area behind the bars is the cumulative probability that the high price for the day has been reached.

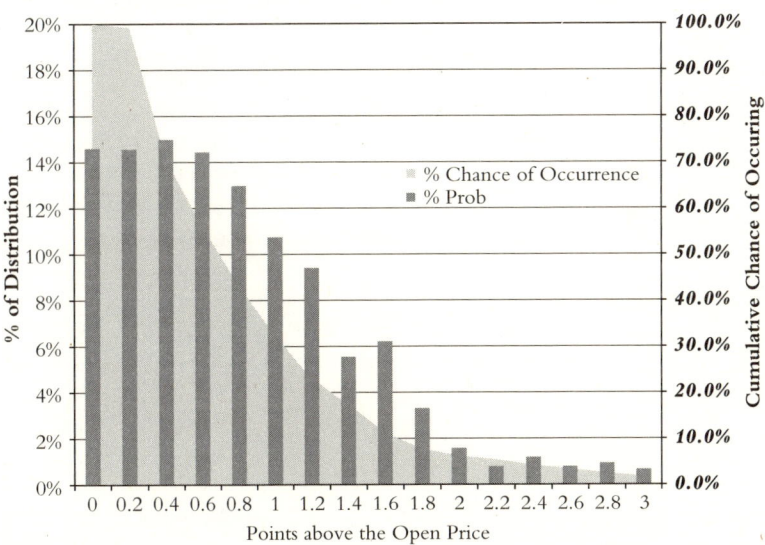

Figure 2.9 Distribution of Price Action above the Opening Price

Figure 2.9 shows the number of times the difference between the *high* and the *opening price* was between each bar, which in this case was 0.2 points. Table 2.6 is the same set of data in tabular form. Presenting this kind of data in two different ways is instructive, as it shows you options of how you can organize it to best fit your style. My preference is to see the numbers; yours may not be. Build the tool that works best for you.

This data becomes a handy cheat sheet for you to use when trading. It is also predictive to a known degree of error. These calculations can be performed on data obtained free from any number of sites like Yahoo! Finance and imported directly into a spreadsheet. If you want to perform a more nuanced statistical regression of the data, please be my guest, but my overarching point is that there are powerful tools at your disposal and you don't need a PhD in statistics. Simply importing a huge data set into a spreadsheet like Excel and running a histogram distribution on the data can yield a clear picture of your odds of getting a particular return on a trade.

Table 2.6 Moves above the Open in Tabular Form

Points below Open	Frequency (N=755)	% Probability Of Occurring
0.2	113	85.40%
0.4	113	70.50%
0.6	107	56.00%
0.8	99	43.00%
1	70	32.30%
1.2	50	22.90%
1.4	38	17.40%
1.6	39	11.10%
1.8	30	7.80%
2	20	6.20%
2.2	18	5.40%
2.4	13	4.20%
2.6	8	3.40%
2.8	10	2.50%
3	6	1.90%

The Conditions of Change

These kinds of statistics help in deciding when to exit a trade as well as monitoring for potential reversals in price. We will cover both of these concepts later in the book.

The next tool you will need is the opposite distribution: the *open* minus the *low*. Both of these sets of statistics tell you the probability of the SPY moving a specific amount each and every day. So now you know that on average any move greater than $0.93 above the open or $0.95 below the open is a low-probability occurrence. Figure 2.10 has the distribution for the price action below the open.

Notice how often the low price is the open price in this example: more than 20 percent of the time. That means one in five days will open at a price *guaranteed* to reverse. By the way, it's similar when the high is the open, which occurs 18.5 percent of the time.

Let's revisit the concept of the inside day and bring that into the discussion here. Each day or bar gives you the opportunity to ask the question as to what the probability is that the next bar will surpass the previous bar's high or low. We've talked about this in the context of the day so far. In the data set used in Figure 2.10, which represented 384 days of trading

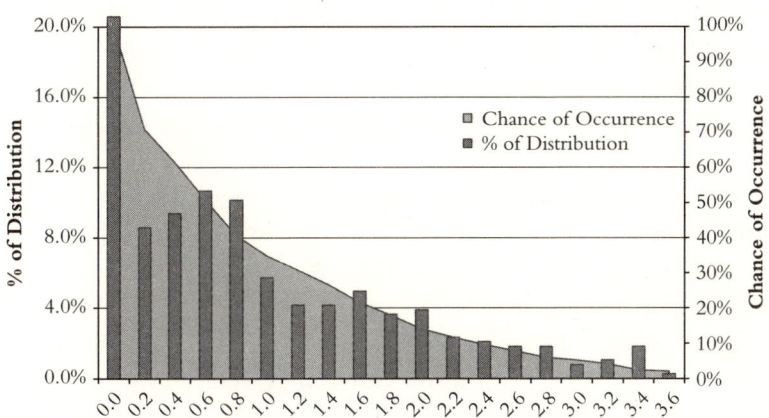

Figure 2.10 Moves below the Open Chart for SPY

Table 2.7 Daily Statistics for SPY

	% Probability	Size of Move
Range		$1.83
Break Previous High	48.20%	
Break Previous Low	43.00%	
Open = High	18.50%	$1.96
Open = Low	20.60%	($1.66)
Break High + Low	5.7%	$1.98

of the SPY ETF, 14.6 percent of the days were inside days, meaning that neither the previous day's high nor low was breached. Conversely, just 5.8 percent of all those days saw *both* the previous high and low breached within the same day.

So now we've constructed a bit of a picture of how the stock will trade during a day. We know that on average it won't move more than $1.00 from the opening price, and that 85 percent of the time, it will break the previous day's high or low. Table 2.7 has a few more statistics about this data set.

Range is simply the average range of the day, the high minus the low. "Break Previous High" shows the percent probability that the previous day's high will be broken, while "Break Previous Low" shows the percent probability that the previous day's low will be broken. "Open = High" is the probability that the open price will be the high for the day and the amount of movement away from that price that will occur on average, (i.e., it will drop $1.96 at some point during that day); "Open = Low" shows the same thing only for the low. "Break High + Low" is the probability that both the high and the low will be broken in the same day as well as the average range of that day.

These are incredibly powerful statistics. They tell you nearly everything you need to know about the stock's behavior on a daily basis. You know that 94 percent of the time after there has been a break of either the previous high or the low, the other one (e.g., the unbroken high/low) will not be broken that day. Moreover, if the stock opens outside of the previous day's range there is a high probability that it will reverse during the day for some very easy money to grab intraday.

When we run these same studies on the weekly trading data and combine it with the daily, we can begin to see where potentially stronger areas of support and resistance will arise. For example, the average range for the week on SPY is $4.20. So if we're looking at three days in a row where offers on balance have been lifted, and the stock has moved $2.20 above the open (the average is $2.03), and the range for the week so far has been $4.00, then it's a good bet that there's not much more money to be gained in this move and the high for the week is very likely near.

This is not the end of the system, but rather the beginning. To review, what we have done here is follow these six steps:

1. Grab historical data for a stock of interest.
2. Perform basic statistics on its behavior to understand the limits of its movement in a given day with respect to the opening price.
3. Calculate the probability of breaking the previous day's high or low.
4. Calculate how far the stock will likely move if it does break the high or low.
5. Note opportunities for rare days and their potential for big moves in the opposite direction.
6. Perform the same set of activities for longer (or shorter) time periods: weekly, monthly, annually.

The last set of statistics you need is the distribution of the size of the stock's moves per day. It is one thing to know the average range; that is very important.

But it is central to this system to know to a certainty the probability of your stock moving a particular amount during a given day. Figure 2.11 differs from Figure 2.9 because it is showing the number of times the SPY has moved *at least* that far, in this case 0.1 points; whereas Figure 2.9 details the number of times the stocks reached a high *between* each successive price bin. Figure 2.11 is saying that 51.6 percent of the time, for example, SPY will move at least 0.6 points above the open. Figure 2.9 is saying that 14.4 percent of the time, the high price will fall between 0.6 and 0.8 points. It's a subtle difference, but it's one that can help you find sweet spots where more money is available in a trade. Figure 2.12 shows the same information for a move down.

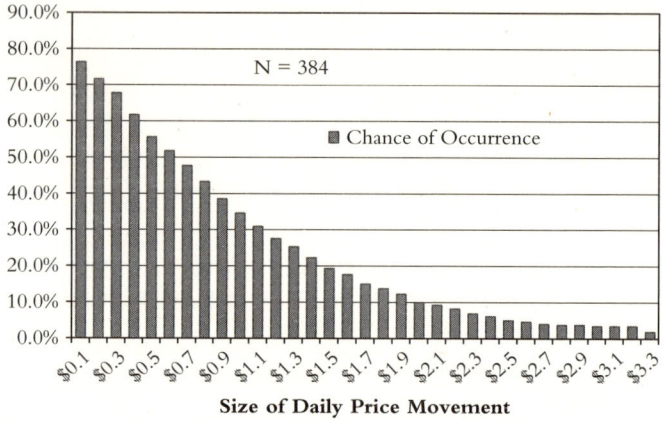

Figure 2.11 SPY Probability Distribution of a Move Up

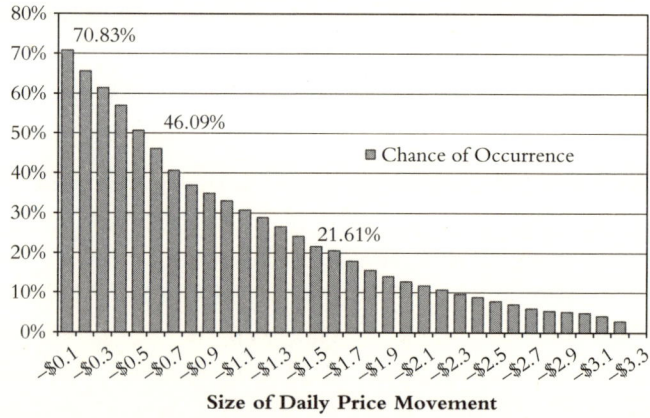

Figure 2.12 SPY Probability Distribution of a Move Down

The Conditions of Change 61

With these statistics, you can now answer the most important question after you've decided to make your move and take a position in a stock, long or short: *What is the probability that I will make X amount of money on this trade?*

Summary

- Staying clear of interpretation creates a cleaner, more ordered mind and one receptive to outlier information when trading.
  - Simplifying your approach to trading is essential to keeping your mind focused on the task at hand.
  - Build simple tools that convey lots of meaning.
- There are four prices that matter (i.e., the high, low, open, and close) because they are definable for a given slice of time.
  - The *high* and the *low* create natural boundaries to the current trading activity, traditionally known as resistance and support.
  - The *open* has the most chaos associated with it because of information since the close that the market has not had a chance to assimilate.
  - The *close* is the most important price because it is the *put up or shut up* price.
    - Institutional players are also very active during the close.
- Creating simple back-tests of a stock's past performance begins to build a database of probabilities for the stock in question.
  - Outside versus inside days: 80 to 90 percent of trading days are outside days.
- Mondays and Fridays tend to trade very differently than the other three days of the week.
  - Back-testing that data for your stock is a good idea.
  - Auction market theory (AMT) breaks the market into two states:
    - Trending or consolidating.
  - Raw volume is of little value.

- Most volume is noise and happens when a stock is not moving.
- The only volume that matters is the volume that lifts offers or hits bids.
- Volume delta information helps you identify when that is happening.
* The opening range is the central concept of the trading system. It defines where potentially high probability trending moves occur.
  * It is classically defined as a slice of time during a trading session or as a consolidation period.
* Defining how far a stock is capable of moving in a particular time period is the next building block.
  * In combination with averages, moves above and below the opening price can reveal the probability of a potential move and refine your entrance timing.
  * The statistics allow you to begin asking questions in ways that yield strong probabilities.

ically faster. This means that the market will drift, chop, and trend again, usually in that order. It is a pattern of consistency and repetition, the back and forth of the charts that repeats itself constantly.

Within this system, a move from the long side is a signal that the market is in a trending mode and will very likely, in the short term, move to a drifting phase, and then a chopping phase, and then look to enter into a new trend. Sometimes the new trend will reverse; that is perfectly acceptable. Sometimes the market will simply continue in its current direction. Therefore, after we have taken a long trade on a breakout of the opening range, we can assume that chop is next, and on most days we can expect a pullback.

Chapter 3

Wax On, Wax Off

Simplicity is the ultimate sophistication.
—*Leonardo DaVinci*

What Goes Around Comes Around

In the Chapter 2 we introduced the tools you will need to begin implementing this system. In getting to this point we've made the argument against traditional technical analysis, brought up some of the limitations of a purely fundamental approach, and begun to challenge the definition of the opening range and how it can be applied, but there is one last thing that we need to go over, one last leap of intuition we have to make. In the end, we have to take the idea of the opening range to its logical conclusion, and in doing so transform it into the core of your activity while trading. The opening range can be thought of as an initial slice of price, not just time.

The classic definition of the opening range is that of a slice of time: the first 30 minutes of a day, the first day of the week, the first week of the month. There's nothing wrong with that definition; I still use it from time to time as a means to generate questions to ask of the market. But I've found that it is more powerful to transform the opening range into a slice of price within the context of a particular period of time.

If you think about it, all definitions of the opening range based on time are completely arbitrary, but in order for your approach to trading to be maximally successful it has to be observationally neutral, meaning that you can't choose a 15-minute opening range one day because you *feel* it's the right thing to do, then use a 30-minute opening range on another day because of a similar *feeling*. If trading needs you to be adaptable, your strategy should be adaptable to the minimum probability of success you are willing to tolerate (e.g., 65 percent, 85 percent, etc.). You can't achieve that with a time-based opening range.

The only way to do that is with a price-based opening range. By defining the opening range based on a change in price within a bar, you can then accurately quantify, based on the stock's past performance, what the probability is of achieving a particular price target within that time period.

This approach will allow you to ask that question I keep bringing up:

If this stock goes up X dollars, what is the probability that it will go up Y dollars?

In Figure 2.8 in Chapter 2, we looked at a monthly chart of Apple (AAPL) and nominated the entire month of January 2004 as the *opening range* for our study.

On a monthly chart, this reduces January 2004 to just one bar; however, if we know all of the statistics of AAPL's behavior for a single month, then we don't need to limit ourselves to only monthly data and time frames. While we are looking at things from a monthly perspective, we can still drill down and watch weekly or daily statistics for clues. Sometimes the action within a week will telegraph a major move from the monthly perspective is about to take place.

Table 3.1 presents the statistics for AAPL on a monthly basis. The first column asks, "How many times did Apple move up at least $0.XX over the open price for the month?" Since our data set was for 42 months, we can see that 40 times out of 42—95.2 percent—Apple moved up at least $0.10 over the open during the month.

Each row on the table indicates the probability that the price will go up by another $0.10. For example, there is a 97.4 percent chance that if the price moved up $0.20 during the month, it will move up $0.30 (highlighted on chart).

Table 3.1 is even more powerful because it can also calculate the probability of a move from any price to any other price. It can answer the question "If the price moves up $0.20 what is the probability that the price moves up $0.70?" If you multiply each of the intervening probabilities then you will have your final probability. But, as powerful as that is, there is

Table 3.1 Probability Calculator: AAPL Example

Price Move	# of Times	# Probability	Log Probability
$0.00	42	1	0.000
$0.10	40	95.2%	−0.021
$0.20	38	95.0%	−0.022
$0.30	37	97.4%	−0.012
$0.40	37	100.0%	0.000
$0.50	35	94.6%	−0.024
$0.60	34	97.1%	−0.013
$0.70	32	94.1%	−0.026
$0.80	31	96.9%	−0.014
$0.90	28	90.3%	−0.044
$1.00	28	100.0%	0.000

an even more elegant way of performing any calculation on the difference between any two numbers.

> **Volume Delta**
>
> The difference between the amount of volume transacted on the bid price versus the ask price. A positive delta implies more offers being lifted, with transactions heavier on the ask. A negative delta implies more bids being hit, with transactions heavier on the bid.

Open a new Excel file and create two columns where you will enter your opening range and your price target. In the next column, create a cell that calculates the number of times the price did not exceed the opening range. To do this, use a COUNTIF function. Looking again at Table 3.1, this data appears in the column labeled "# of Times." COUNTIF scans an entire data set and counts the number of cells where the value of the cell *does not match your criteria*. So make your criteria less than or equal to your opening range:

$$\text{COUNTIF (Range, price} =< \text{opening range)}$$
$$\text{Full Excel syntax: =COUNTIF}$$
$$(\$column\$1:\$column\$100,"<="\&opening\ range)$$

where:
$column$1:$column$100 = the *High – Open* column in your spreadsheet for 100 data points.
"<="& *opening range* = the criteria. (The operator <= must be in quotation marks and the cell reference must be joined to it with the &.)

In Figure 3.1, the cells under the "What If?" column are highlighted. The first two cells contain the opening range (2.5) and the price target (5). In another column of this particular spreadsheet (not shown), I have calculated a set of data that

	% Probability	# of Points			
Range		9.94	**Up Move**	*What If?*	# of times
Avg. High Move		4.66	Opening Range	2.5	151
Break Prev High	56.0%		Target Move	5	86
Avg. Low Move		−5.28	% Probability	56.95%	
Break Prev. Low	27.3%				
Total Breaks	97.6%		**Down Move**	*What If?*	# of times
Inside Day	6.7%		Opening Range	−4	127
High + Low Break	4.4%	9.63	Target Move	−6.33	77
Open is High	0.4%	−5.6	% Probability	60.63%	
Open is Low	0.0%	#DIV/0!			

Figure 3.1 Example of Using COUNTIF to Calculate Probabilities

represents the high minus the low price. COUNTIF tells me that, in that data set, the high has exceeded the open (i.e., the opening range) by 2.5 points or less 151 times. In the "Target Move" cell I've done the same calculation only using the price target of 5 points, which happened 86 times. By dividing 151 into 86, I obtain the result 0.5695 or 56.95 percent, which is calculated in cell labeled "% Probability."

Now we can combine this knowledge with the current action of the volume. Remember, in auction market theory (AMT) we are looking for the volume that moves the market. We can use the volume deltas to relay this information to us. So while day traders will need to buy specialized software that grabs that data in real time for moment to moment changes in the market's behavior, we can use freely available daily and weekly data to do the same thing here, re-creating the moment when AAPL began its breakout and set out on a historic run up in price over three years.

Figure 3.2 shows the volume delta data for AAPL on a monthly basis. Note that for many of the months leading up to the breakout, the volume was slightly bearish, as there was more selling than there was buying. The supply of sellers was, on balance, higher than the supply of buyers.

That changed, however beginning in February 2004, where the selling reached its peak during the week of January 16, and buyers began to outnumber sellers. Figure 3.3 has the data. It also shows how the huge volume spike on March 5 was capable

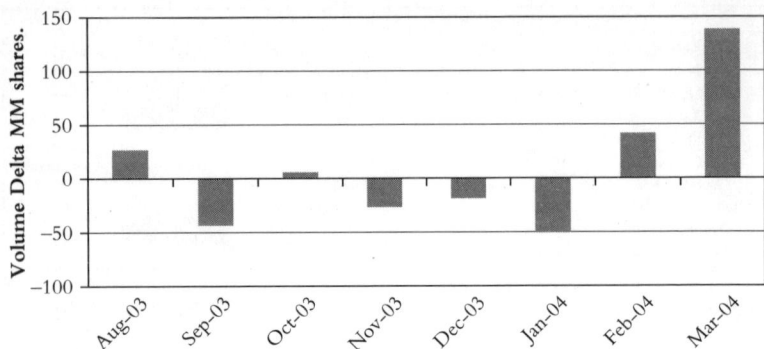

Figure 3.2 Volume Delta Example for AAPL, Monthly

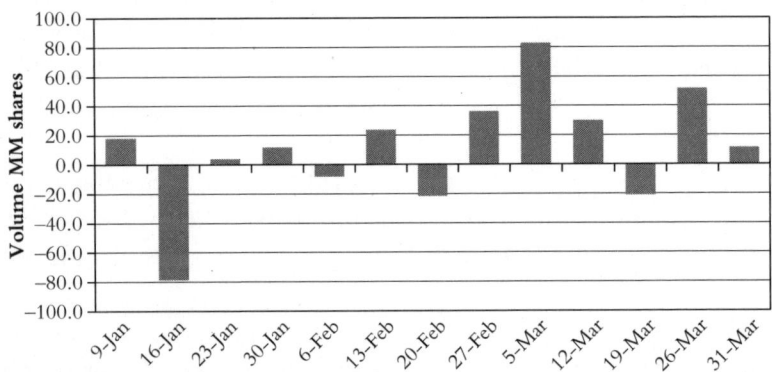

Figure 3.3 Volume Delta Example for AAPL, Weekly (2004)

of lifting the price out of its two-month-long consolidation. So here we have a perfect example of using the volume delta to help us determine not only the timing of our entry into the market, but also why we really do not need to arbitrarily define the opening range as a particular moment in time (e.g., the beginning of a year, month, hour, etc.). In essence, the opening range can be simply the beginning of a bar itself.

Note how in Figure 3.3 there is a huge negative volume delta the week ending January 16, 2004, which corresponds

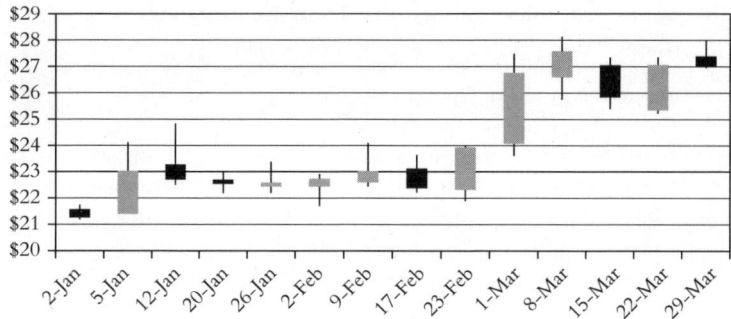

Figure 3.4 Weekly Chart of AAPL (2004)

with a negative bar. This was volume that attempted to move the market but was incapable of doing so. The buyers could not overcome the sellers and the price pulled back into a range. Then, during the week of March 1, shown in Figure 3.4, nearly the same amount of volume delta was capable of moving the market above that level and the stock never looked back.

In this case, even though we were looking to trade AAPL from a monthly perspective, we could drill into the weekly or even daily trading action to gain more clarity as to what is happening to refine our entry point.

Building on this idea and looking again at Figure 2.8 (Chapter 2) and some monthly statistics about AAPL (Table 3.2), we can make the following observations.

In February, the high was $24.10 and the month's closing price was $23.92, and the opening price on March 1 was $24.10. So with this information let's construct a question that will help us define both our opening range and our price target:

If the price of Apple in March moves up $0.10, what is the probability that it will move up $1.00 before the end of the month?

Having constructed a monthly set of statistics similar to the ones in Chapter 2 (Figure 2.11), I know the answer is 70.0 percent. There are four reasons why I asked this particular question:

Table 3.2 Relevant Statistics Describing a Stock

Range	$4.11
Average Move above Open?	$2.09
Average Move below Open?	−$2.02
Probability of Breaking Prev. High?	50.00%
Probability of Breaking Prev. Low?	35.71%
Chance of Inside Month	21.43%
Probability of Breaking High & Low?	7.14%

1. The difference between the opening price for the month and the February high is $0.00. March opened at the February high, giving a high probability that the February high would be broken.
2. The stock was in a bullish position because the open for March was higher than the close for February.
3. There's a 93 percent chance that the stock will not break the February low then, which limits my downside risk to $21.70.
4. I also know that if the stock moves up $0.10, breaking the previous month's high that it has a 70 percent chance of moving up $1.00.

In my question, I am defining the first criteria for movement, $0.10, as my opening range. I'm asking: If my opening range is $0.10 and that range is broken to the upside, then what is the probability of the stock reaching my target price? Figure 3.5 visualizes this concept.

Once it reaches my target price, I can ask a similar question, this time redefining the opening range as $1.00:

If the stock moves up $1.00, what is the probability of the stock going up $1.50?

The answer is even better; it's 78.6 percent, in this case. And I can rest easier knowing that my position has strengthened during the course of the move up from $24.10 to $25.10 as opposed to being fearful of there being a reversal at that moment. Now the average move up above the opening price is just over $2.00, so I would keep that in mind and note the

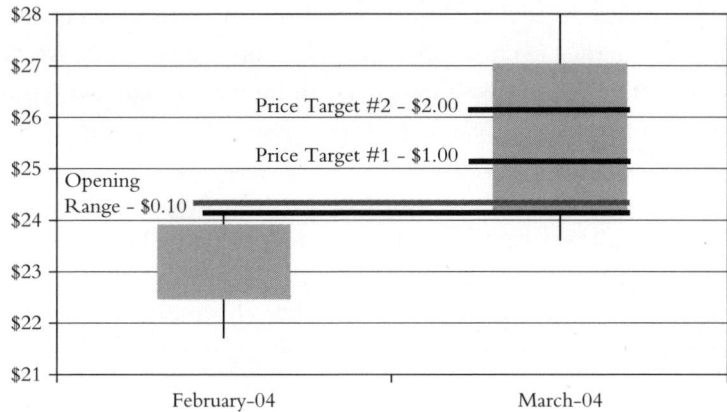

Figure 3.5 Opening Range as a Slice of a Bar for AAPL

volume deltas on a daily or weekly basis and decide to lighten up the position and let my profits ride.

Even though this was an explosive month for Apple, the range was only slightly higher than the four-year average of $4.11. The low was $23.60 and the high was $28.14 (range of $4.54), but it was nearly all above the opening price. The volume deltas told us this was the start of a trending move and our statistics confirmed that this setup had a high probability of succeeding, which it did.

It's Always Noon Somewhere

Now that you have an example of how I approach a particular trade, I thought it would be valuable to go over what my typical trading day is like. I started trading futures first as an individual investor and then professionally, landing jobs with trading firms in Toronto and New York, doing quite well in applying my studies to the market. Those were great times for me, between 2004 and 2007, and I saw the hard work pay off handsomely.

Opening ranges and their relationship to the previous day's range form the framework of the potential trade, but it is not as simple as that. No matter how in tune we think we are with current events and their effect on the markets, we are not machines. While we sleep, everything we thought we knew may have been rendered worthless because a decision was made or a report was released.

That said, my trading morning actually begins before I go to sleep. It's then that I look to review metrics like momentum, volatility, and general trends, with an eye toward detecting extremes: The more extreme the market sentiment and trend in a particular direction, the greater the probability of a reversal once the macro condition that caused that sentiment is lifted.

I like to look qualitatively at the market, noting broad technical indicators and asking questions such as:

- Is the market making higher highs?
- Are corrections losing steam before reaching the previous low?
- Was yesterday's close bullish or bearish?
- Was there a breakout/down? If so, was volume extremely high or low?

Doing this will give me a context for what I saw while watching the ticker during trading and provide some idea of what may happen in the morning.

For example, recent headlines have been dominated by the questionable solvency of several eurozone countries and their ability to continue servicing their sovereign debt. This has cast a huge pall over all of the markets, from the United States to the Pacific Rim. No market has been insulated from the fear generated by this situation and any news that would be perceived as a solution to the problem would be met with a violent reversal of direction, as investors would be willing to put their money at risk again. The length and strength of the reversal would be dependent on the magnitude of the news. In markets like these, trading becomes very difficult, so constant review is critical.

With the evening chores done, I can go to sleep with a clear conscience and allow my subconscious to process everything I took in during the day. Upon waking up, I go through my morning routine of checking how the Asian and European markets have traded and looking for signs of increased volatility. A quick perusal of the overnight U.S. Globex market and comparing it with the previous day's range precedes a brief review of the headlines in the *Wall Street Journal* and the *Financial Times*.

After that it's a review of pre-market data relevant to the day's trading, while trying to integrate how the market is reacting to various government economic reports in both Europe and the United States. By this point, data saturation is setting in and my brain is full. If this sounds like a lot to do in order to make a trade, it can be—especially if events are moving quickly. Often the timing of the release of certain information is critical to how the market absorbs it. You will not become an expert overnight, but don't let that scare you. Being able to organize all of this data in real time is a skill, and like all skills, it needs to be practiced through repetition. Learning how to collect and organize data is something that adds to your edge through time.

After all that, it's time to watch the market. This is where simplicity of design in the trading system pays dividends. There are all of these macro-market conditions to get caught up on, but they only create the background of the picture—whether it's like an active volcano or a pastoral meadow. The charts for the day are going to draw themselves in over this background, filling in the details that make up the bulk of the picture.

Market watching begins around 8:30 a.m. Eastern Standard Time, with the opening of New York futures pit trading. I don't typically trade here. During this hour before the New York market opens, I can get a pretty firm grip on the setting and can estimate whether we'll be trading in a range and how much volatility we're likely to see.

The next step is forming a hypothesis about the market. While scientists may take months or years to find a question worth asking, traders have opportunities to ask questions every minute. In the early stages of your trading it may be a good exercise to write down your hypotheses; that way you will have something tangible to review at the end of the day.

They can be as time specific as this:

If XYZ Corp. can hold above the 3 a.m. low, which tracked well with the DAX (Deutsche Borse AG German Stock Index), we have a good chance of breaking above yesterday's high price.

Or as general as this:

If the S&P closes below the opening range of the year we have an increased likelihood of entering a downtrend.

Obviously major news events, earthquakes, wars, central bank communications, and elections also have enormous impact on the markets and will force reassessment of my hypotheses on the fly.

Once the markets open, I tend to watch the ticker very closely, looking for signs of large traders entering or leaving the market. If I'm looking to go long, then I like to wait for selling to hit and note how well the price stood versus a key reference point. If I'm inclined to short the market, the converse is true: I'm looking for buying to see how much conviction the bulls have and whether they can push the price through a particular price level. I want to follow the market after a move in a particular direction has exhausted itself. In common trader parlance this is called *fading a move*. You wait for the current trend to play itself out and, because of your fundamental or statistical analysis of the situation, you put on a contrarian position looking for an easy gain.

More often than not, my trades revolve around a test of the ranges we went over in Chapter 1 and breakouts with respect to their moving up or down. In other words, I don't go into the market with both guns blazing while everyone else is shooting; I'd rather wait for the dust to settle and pick up what pieces are left afterward. That's the point of establishing a classic, time-based opening range: to let the less disciplined market operators finish their calisthenics and then, when the market has established a bias and a range, look for an opportunity to make a trade.

I have become very picky, and many times will not even put on a trade if conditions don't present themselves; or I will take only small, exploratory positions. If there's no good opportunity to make money, then forcing the matter won't help you profit. Don't feel that you need to be involved in a trade at all times. Sometimes the best move to make is to not make one at all.

Trading isn't chess.

Most of the moves the markets make are just noise, and they can and will be a source of confusion. You set the terms of your involvement. You can always walk away from the ticker if the market is confusing you. As a matter of fact, I recommend it.

Confusion means that your brain is overloaded or distracted. Good decisions can never come during a heightened emotional or confused state. Sometimes it is best to walk away from the market and do something that is completely unrelated to it: watch a movie, play a game with your child, clean the garage, and so on. I know some people who exercise, take a long walk, do yoga, or meditate. What's important to remember is that the markets are always there to present you with another opportunity to make some money, so do not lament any missed opportunities because you took the day off.

Back to the trading day; if my current hypothesis is proving correct and the market is moving my way, I may double down on my analysis by buying a block of stock that is complementary to my original position. In an active day, I may make many small trades.

While *opening-range–style* trading is often thought of only in terms of day-trading—the context I'm using it in here—that does not mean it cannot be adapted to longer time frames. As we've already discussed, the opening range is a concept that is just as applicable to a week or month as it is to a day or an hour.

As far as the mechanics of the trade itself, if my hypothesis proves incorrect, I will cut the position off at my predetermined level (known as a *stop*) and walk away from the trade with a small loss. Losses are almost always more insightful than gains, as they force you to reassess your assumptions. While I'm not here to argue the merits of her work or philosophy, Ayn Rand is famous for a phrase that every trader should always keep in the back of his or her head: "Check your premises."

While this is happening, I review my trades and will always review a losing trade before placing another one. If I can't figure out why the trade went against me I'll usually stop trading for the day. Obviously my premises are wrong and I have not taken sufficient time to figure out what the correct ones are. My purpose in doing this is twofold, especially on losing trades: The first is to glean what the trade told me about the market, and the second is to learn how to improve my execution. Taking the time to do this is a valuable exercise and helps me avoid mistakes due to emotion while things are moving quickly. I always review my profit/loss and the growth rate of my account—to the penny, without fail.

So there it is in a few paragraphs—a typical day for me when day-trading the markets. Distilled into seven steps it involves:

1. Research on the stock and the general state of the market, including what its bias was the previous day in relation to its pre-opening state.
2. Creating hypotheses about ranges, potential breakouts, and the moves that will capture value.
3. Noting whether the stock is making a new high for the day, week, month, quarter, or year.
4. Tracking real-time waves of buying and selling; keeping track of volume delta in relation to price.
5. Identifying the potential breadth of a range and/or significant price levels.
6. Exiting a losing trade without ego.
7. Reviewing endlessly where I went right and wrong.

This routine is designed as a path to continued improvement of both my method and my performance. The more comfortable you can be with the information you have acquired, the more confident you can be in your decision making. Profit and loss, as in any entrepreneurial venture, are measures of how well you've served your customer.

Since you're the customer when trading, you ultimately serve yourself.

Opening Range Jitters

Unlike in other forms of business, in trading the customer is not always right. You will make bad trades. The goal of this approach to trading is to identify high probability setups and act on them and nothing else. The markets are extremely treacherous and this approach is both aggressive and defensive at the same time. It's defensive because there is very little guesswork. It's almost mechanical—dare I say, *algorithmic*—once you get used to it.

In the end, the markets are dominated by high-frequency trading systems and their algorithms. In a way, the beginnings of the system I outlined at the beginning of this chapter simply form your algorithm. It's a flow chart of reading and reacting to new data.

When I trade this system I do so from no smaller than a 30-minute time frame. You may find that shorter or longer time frames work for you but I use 30 minutes because that's where I find myself working at the limits of my attention and energy. So I'm breaking the day down into 30-minute segments. I have the statistics in front of me that I showed you in Table 3.1, along with a spreadsheet capable of calculating on the fly the probability of a trade based on the numbers I put into it as each new bar forms.

Tip

Start by looking at stocks from a daily perspective and watch how they trade. That's where the best and lowest-cost data is available.

	% Probability	# of Points			
Range		11.06	Up Move	*What If?*	# of times
Avg. High Move		5.10	Opening Range	0.77	107
Break Prev High	51.5%		Target Move	3	75
Avg. Low Move		−5.96	% Probability	70.09%	
Break Prev. Low	37.1%				
Total Breaks	88.6%		*Down Move*	*What If?*	# of times
Inside Day	12.9%		Opening Range	−6	46
High + Low Break	5.3%	Avg Move	Target Move	−10	28
Open is High	0.0%	11.7	% Probability	60.87%	
Open is Low	0.8%	#DIV/0!			

Uptrend Length	# of Times	Reversal %	Downtrend Length	# of Times	Reversal %
1	28		−1	27	
2	18	35.7%	−2	11	59.3%
3	13	27.8%	−3	8	27.3%
4	6	53.8%	−4	4	50.0%
5	3	50.0%	−5	1	75.0%
6	2	33.3%	−6	1	0.0%
7	2		−7	1	

Figure 3.6 Spreadsheet Example, AAPL Weekly Data

Figure 3.6 is an example of a spreadsheet of the relevant numbers for AAPL, calculated on a weekly basis; all of the fields in it are explained in detail in Appendix B: Building a Trade. It looks like a lot of data, but really there are only a few numbers here that come to bear for each bar. I work in 30-minute intervals because it gives me time to absorb what is happening at the beginning of each new bar, formulate some hypotheses, test them, and still have time to think about the other things that are going on: checking the weekly or monthly charts to see this move in relation to those time scales, review the previous day's action, and so on. It also allows for enough time to get up and grab a cup of coffee or quick bite to eat.

Figure 3.6 contains all the statistics we've calculated previously along with the probability of success for a target move. The bottom section calculates the odds of potential longer-term reversals, based on past behavior and the length of the run. In this instance, if Apple has been up at the end of three consecutive weeks, there is a 63.6 percent chance of a reversal in the fourth week.

Regardless of what time frame you pick, the rules for how to use the opening range remain the same:

- Stocks trading above the previous bar's closing price are in a bullish posture.
- Stocks trading below the previous bar's closing price are in a bearish posture.
- When the previous bar's high or low is breached, your opening range is going to be the open of this bar plus the high or low of the previous bar.
- Your target will be the average move in that direction from the open.
- Volume deltas provide support for your probabilities by showing who has the upper hand, buyers or sellers.

Once the stock has moved away from the opening range, it's time to focus on the criteria that will help you determine the probabilities of hitting the target price.

Use breakouts based on earlier highs and lows to anticipate the momentum of the stock as it moves away from the opening range towards a reversal point. Your statistics and the hypothesis that you tested will give you your odds. These previous highs and lows—especially if there is significant volume historically associated with them—become significant intraday price levels, and therefore can be used to good effect to create hypotheses and test them as the bars of the day or week develop.

Let's take our example of AAPL's breakout and go through it step by step using Figure 3.7.

Figure 3.7 is a daily chart (A) with the volume delta (B). Near the beginning of the chart is March 1, which is both the

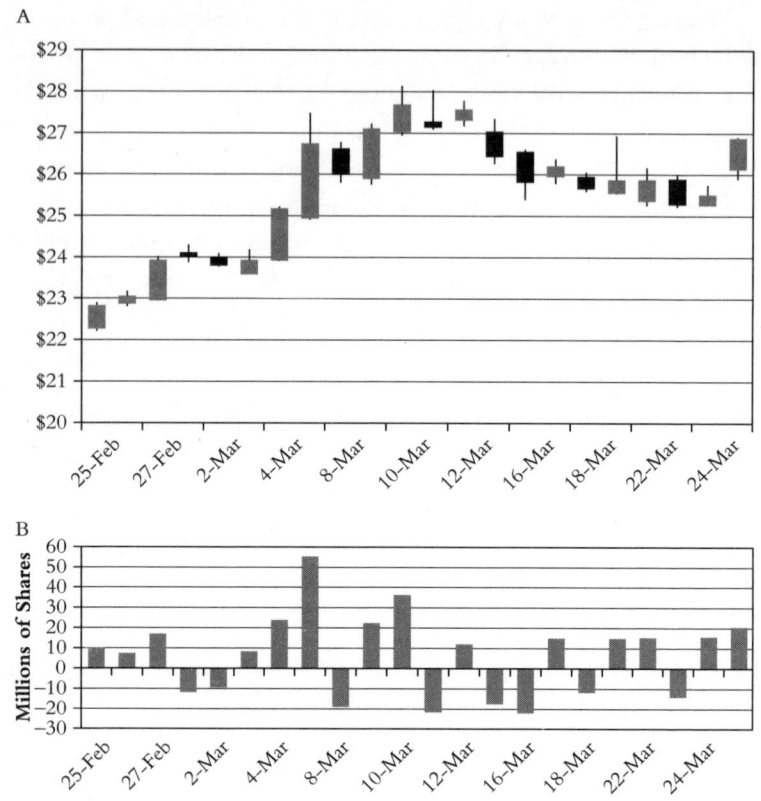

Figure 3.7 Daily Chart of AAPL in March 2004 Breakout (A) and Volume Delta (B)

beginning of the month and the week. We're trading this from a monthly basis. On the morning of March 1, AAPL opens at $24.10, above the previous daily close and daily high, and equal to February's monthly high. Probabilities are good that we will break the previous month's high—it only has to go up a penny, after all. We are in a bullish posture because the three previous daily volume deltas were all positive. Knowing this before hitting the market, we can ask the question:

If Apple goes up $0.10 what is the probability that Apple will go up $1.00?

The answer is 70 percent; so I'm waiting for $24.20 to happen. If it's achieved during the month, I know I have a 70 percent chance of making $0.90 by the end of the month—and it happens that day. AAPL hits a high of $24.30 that day but sells off slightly. I'm not very worried because in four years AAPL has never broken both the previous monthly high (which it's already done) and the previous monthly low. I'm in the stock at $24.20 and my absolute downside target is $21.70, the February 2004 monthly low, which is highly unlikely.

March 2 opens slightly below the previous day's close ($24.02) at $24.00. (See Table 3.3.) A slightly bearish posture is warranted, but no worry exists because our monthly downside target is $21.70 and the average weekly range is $1.60 (Figure 3.6). There is a high probability that AAPL will not fall below $22.50 this week. During the day it drops below the previous day's low of $23.87 and closes at $23.81, making for an outside day that is completely normal given the way the stock opened and our statistics. Both of these down days have happened with a below-average range for the day at $0.60, indicating that there is no conviction to the selling. After the false breakout on the monthly open, the chart shows consolidation-type behavior.

March 3 opens below the March 2 low, at $23.60. This turns out to be the low of the day and Apple moves higher

Table 3.3 Daily Trading Data for AAPL in 2004

Date	Open	High	Low	Close	Volume
27-Feb	22.96	24.02	22.95	23.92	16,744,200
1-Mar	24.1	24.3	23.87	24.02	11,488,600
2-Mar	24	24.1	23.77	23.81	9,167,400
3-Mar	23.6	24.19	23.6	23.92	8,040,400
4-Mar	23.93	25.22	23.91	25.16	23,579,400
5-Mar	24.95	27.49	24.9	26.74	55,021,400
8-Mar	26.62	26.79	25.8	26	18,674,000

on positive volume delta and below-average total volume, meaning there are very few sellers left in the market. The range is normal, $0.59, suggesting buyers are getting the upper hand.

March 4 opens right at the previous day's close. There is no bias to the market; it is completely neutral. The previous day's high and low are around $0.30 away from the open. But buyers come in and lift bids all day with the low dipping just slightly below the open and the stock takes off through $24.20 and achieves the original price target of $25.10 (if up $0.10, will it go up $1.00 from $24.10 per share).

Thursday's high of $25.22 and close of $25.16 on massive volume is an excellent signal, and it allows us to ask a new question of the market:

If Apple has gone up $1.00 what is the probability it will go up $2.00?

The answer is barely better than even odds at 53.7 percent. Looking a little further out, however, the statistics also showed that every time AAPL went up $2.00, it went up $2.60. Knowing that my odds are now a toss-up to grab the next $1.60, I hold what I have and wait to see if the volume delta the next day indicates selling action. The average weekly range, $1.60, has been achieved so that should be worrisome because on more selling it would create a high probability of an intraday reversal of some amount. It would be prudent to sell into the day's high and consider a pullback next week.

Friday March 5 opens down slightly, but quickly reverses and rockets higher, hitting my next price target of $26.10. I then have to ask the next question:

If Apple has gone up $2.00 what's the probability it will go up $3.00?

For the month, probability is 73.3 percent, but it's just 11.1 percent for the week. Since it's already gone up $1.00 that day, there is only a 10 percent chance that it will go up another $1.00 that day. If I'm watching the ticker because this is such abnormal behavior, I have to decide between playing for reversal and accumulating on a pullback next week, or just holding onto what I've bought because AAPL still has not gotten overextended from the very long time frame from which I am trading it, monthly.

As we can see from Table 3.3, Apple hit an intraday high of $27.49 and even the most long-term focused trader would have seen an opportunity to sell into that spike and pick up some stock after a pullback. Day-traders, those focused on the 5- or 10-minute chart, would be going short into that peak in the hope that there would be some easy money, as the stock was very overextended.

With a close of $26.79, there was some money to be made, but with the kind of positive momentum AAPL had at that point, it would be suicide to hold that short over the weekend. That closing price was a weekly close and, as we discussed in Chapter 1, that's a very powerful signal: a massive explosion of buying on a Friday—550 percent of normal volume—most of it by buyers lifting offers.

Going short into that would be not only brave, but also foolish. I'm not a superhero. I don't get fame or money for being brave.

In this example, the daily and weekly action is important for you to use to monitor the behavior of the stock in a cursory way. At the end of March, I would have reviewed the monthly data in the context of the quarterly and annual data in the same way that I just showed you to do between the daily, weekly, and monthly perspectives.

For those who want to manage their investments more actively, focusing on the weekly price movements is a good idea. It means that you can take five minutes at the end of each trading day, look at what happened, glance at your statistics, and know with confidence where your investments are in relation to their historical behavior and whether any action is warranted.

If you are investing at the monthly time frame, looking to hold the stock for a couple of years, then reviewing the price action at the end of each week makes sense. Set your spreadsheet up to grab weekly, monthly, and quarterly data and review it over the weekend.

This system is adaptable to all of these time frames as well as shorter ones. Like I said, when I trade I use the 30-minute bar, as opposed to daily or hourly. If you are the type of person that can handle the 15- or even 5-minute time frame, more power to you. Thirty minutes is what I've found yields my best results.

Objects in Motion

Given that there are a number of ways to approach trading, it stands to reason that everyone uses different combinations of tools to drive their trading decisions. One thing that is a constant for most people is identifying support and resistance levels. AMT would define these levels as the extremes of the new consolidation range. In the end, a majority of traders use similar tools to identify support and resistance and place their bets according to their findings. My goal is, in some ways, to free you from that process so you can focus on identifying resistance or support and not agonize over wondering when it will show up. Trying to anticipate it can lead to too much focus on something that may never occur. Statistics from longer time frames give you some idea of where support and resistance lie, as do previous highs and lows.

There are as many different styles of trading as there are traders; no two traders will see the same support and resistance levels or the boundaries of the current consolidation state in the same way. The push and pull between bears and bulls at the edges of the consolidation range is where the market is saying the most. The opportunity for the price to go higher or lower once the level is breached creates a lot of trading activity, otherwise known as volume.

Markets tend not to hang around very long between support and resistance levels. Quite the opposite happens, actually. Once fair value in a consolidation has been determined, the price oscillations will become more and more muted until almost no activity happens. People don't trade unless they believe they are getting a bargain; if everyone agrees that this price is fair then there is no reason to trade.

The breakout move almost always happens with rapidly increasing volume in a short time frame, with sellers pounding bids or buyers lifting offers. Volume deltas in the minute-to-minute bars are heavily skewed to one side of the market. Once the level is taken out, those who were sitting on the sidelines, the momentum traders, pile in to catch as much of the move as possible. If I'm trading intraday, I'm one of those people. Traders who don't pay up quickly find themselves squeezed out as the market refuses to back up and take them along at even a modest discount of a few pennies.

Breakouts fail all the time, some of them are pure head-fakes or raids on those that have their sell-stops set very tightly. It's important to let the breakout confirm itself by waiting for the bar to close after the price has moved through your opening range.

In the example from the last section, we set an initial opening range of $0.10 because the open to the previous high were identical. In the example, stock was purchased once the price reached the opening range price. But, it turns out that was not the optimal play, and the stock reversed during the day and spent the next two days meandering around below the opening range. Waiting for a daily close above the opening range was the smarter play, especially from the monthly perspective that we were basing our decisions on.

In the hypothesis we tested—*What is the probability of Apple moving up $1.00 if it moved up $0.10?*—I did not mention anything about time. Therefore, going back to the idea that the closing price is the most important price of the day (the *put up or shut up price*) one should not ever be in a hurry to take a position, long or short, until the signal is confirmed by the price closing above your opening range price.

In our example, we would have left the entire first target price on the table, that initial $1.00, because AAPL did not close above $24.20 per share until it closed over $25.00 per share. But in the context of holding the stock for the next three or four years because the fundamentals of the company were so strong, that $1.00 is meaningless to your potential return on the trade, which could have been as much as 900 percent.

Leaving $1 on the table to radically improve your chances of making $175 and not leaving your capital dead in a losing position should not be considered a loss of any sort.

By defining the opening range this way and waiting for a little bit of confirmation, you are drastically improving your chances of taking a position that will break the way you've determined it should.

Imagine you're an old man who spends his mornings sitting on a street corner watching people go through a busy intersection, feeding the proverbial pigeons. There's a coffee shop across the street. Every day you see me walk along this side of the street, up to the corner. Some days I keep on going straight, presumably on my way to work, but some days I turn at the corner to cross the street to get a cup of coffee.

As the observer, you know with a very high degree of probability that, in those first few steps after the turn, I will be going to the coffee shop. In fact, you would be more likely to notice if I didn't grab a cup of coffee than if I went through my routine, since that would be an outlier event and our brains are wired to notice outlier events more than routine ones.

But if you are sitting there with your friend one morning and make a bet that I will show up and go straight through the intersection *before* I do so, you are taking a much bigger risk with your money than if you decided to wait until I took that first step toward the coffee shop.

In a sense, the impetus of motion in a direction is the moment that you want to make your decision; you don't want to anticipate the event happening until it begins to happen. Once it does, then you can proceed with so much more clarity of purpose.

The same thing happens with stocks. If you know that on days when the stock moves a little bit above the open it will most likely move at least a set amount further, that presents a high-probability trade setup for you.

For another example of how this works, Table 3.4 has some statistics on the last two years of the gold futures market. In this case, N=680 days of trading where the high price exceeded the opening price. Only 3.5 percent of the time was the open price the high price for gold in this data set. If you nominate a 0.1 percent rise above the open as the top of your opening range and ask the question:

What is the probability of price rising 0.5 percent after it rises 0.1 percent and breaks the opening range?

Table 3.4 answers 63.2 percent. So you can enter a trade in gold with a 63.2 percent certainty of making 0.4 percent on a trade if the price exceeds the opening price by 0.1 percent. Table 3.4 also tells you that if gold breaks above the open at all, 91.8 percent of the time it will move more than 0.1 percent.

When a range breaks, in my experience, the only winning strategy is to do as I described above with respect to the momentum, and that is to go with the flow until it ends, taking your profit and being satisfied with it. As a general rule, you can expect the trending move following a breakout to last as long as it took for the stock to break out of the previous range. For example, if XYZ Corp. traded between $6.50 and $7.25 per share for a week, you can expect that once the stock convincingly bests $7.25 on strong volume that the trending move will

Table 3.4 Probability of Breadth of Opening Range Breakout

% Rise above Open	# of Days	% of Distribution	% Probability of High after Opening Range Breakout
0.10%	56	8.20%	
0.20%	70	10.30%	89.70%
0.30%	68	10.00%	79.70%
0.40%	59	8.70%	71.00%
0.50%	53	7.80%	63.20%
0.60%	51	7.50%	55.70%

last days and not minutes. Regardless of that observation, which may or not be helpful, reviewing the statistics for greater and greater deviations from the open will tell you when the odds are no longer in your favor.

In the end, it is important when starting out to begin slowly. Find one or two situations, or setups, and master them. Don't mix and match. I don't trade every setup that comes my way. I have a few that I am comfortable with and execute on with a high degree of success. It was in studying a number of different setups that I identified the ones where I was most comfortable, and I still trade only those.

What you are looking for is similar to something that happened in the AAPL trade I outlined in the last section, where the odds were excellent that there would be an opening range breakout to the upside on a very small movement in price. That made a perfect entry point for a high-probability trade. Then as the trade developed and the first price objective was reached my odds of capturing more price appreciation (the move from +$1.00 to +$2.00) went down, but they improved after that (the move from +$2.00 to +$3.00).

Moreover, since the opening-range breakout for the month occurred over a very small total range—$0.60, as compared to an average monthly range of $4.11 (data not shown)—there were even odds that I would see nearly $4.00 of price appreciation that month alone, which is exactly what happened. For a position that cost me $24.20 per share to put on, I had even odds to make $3.51 per share ($4.11 average range minus the difference between my buy point, $24.20, and the low of the month, $23.60) or 14.5 percent gain.

This kind of favorable setup is nearly the closest thing to the perfect storm that you could ask for. It would have been very possible to trade the stock for the easy money within the month, selling and taking your money off the table once it was obvious that the high for the month had been made, and then waiting for the beginning of the next month to look for another trading opportunity. That is just as valid a strategy as identifying the opening-range breakout on March 4 as the beginning of a larger move and holding it until the first monthly reversal took place.

This is the power of defining the opening range in terms of price and not in terms of time. It is possible to trade within a bar and stay completely focused on what is happening now. This leaves you the flexibility to review your position as a good one and be content to let it ride into the next bar. Both are perfectly valid strategies, as is pulling your initial stake off the table (selling) and leaving your profit in the form of stock if you like the chances of its continuing to make you money.

My studies during those two years I spent devouring knowledge and sleeping on Andrew's couch led me to this way of trading. Armed with all of this and a few spreadsheets and crib notes, I was able to go back into the market and do very well. By 2007 my skill led me to spend some time as a prop desk trader in New York and Toronto, and I had amassed a small fortune. Trading had become boring. I had reduced the markets down to an algorithm and while the money and sense of accomplishment were nice, I realized that I wanted to do more than just be an optimal prop trader.

It was at that point that I realized I didn't love trading as much as I loved being an entrepreneur. I succeeded in this entrepreneurial venture. I had a very successful business as a market operator, but it no longer held any challenge and it was time to do something different.

Summary

- The opening range is really a slice of price, not a slice of time.
    - Ask a question: *If the stock goes up X what's the probability it will go up Y?*
    - Creating a spreadsheet that will automatically calculate your probabilities by cutting and pasting publicly available data.
    - Volume delta is also calculable using publicly available data for daily, weekly, and monthly time periods.

- The system is designed to have you ask a new question every time a bar closes based on what just happened.
  - For example: *The stock moved $0.50 above the open, what is the probability it will move $1.00?*
- Cultivate a pre- and post-market routine.
- Follow rules for using the opening range as a slice of price.
  - Stocks trading above the previous bar's closing price are in a bullish posture.
  - Stocks trading below the previous bar's closing price are in a bearish posture.
  - When the previous bar's high or low is breached, your opening range is going to be the open of this bar plus the high or low of the previous bar.
  - Your target will be the average move in that direction from the open.
  - Volume deltas provide support for your probabilities by showing who has the upper hand, buyers or sellers.
- Markets that are consolidating have no direction; the bulls and the bears cannot gain an advantage over each other.
  - Once a high or low is broken, the market moves quickly away from the old range.
  - The opening range as a slice of price is akin to observing a car just beginning to turn right as opposed to left.
  - High probability setups where the open is near the previous high or low are great setups to exploit.

Chapter 4

As the Market Turns...

Opportunities multiply as they are seized.
—*Sun Tzu*

Subconscious Implications

Here I am, having made a lot of money in a relatively short period of time, and I'm becoming bored with it. Money is not an end unto itself; it is a means to an end, and now that I had the means, I had to think about how I could do something with it to create something bigger. Not to be boastful, but life was pretty good at that point. I had made much more money than I had expected and I felt a little bit like I owed the world.

In trading as a profession, it is arguable that you are not creating value but rather simply helping to discover what the real value of a company is. So in that sense, traders perform an extremely valuable service as appraisers of assets, and for that they get paid, but there is nothing lasting about what they produce.

There's no legacy, unless you take what you've earned and build something great with it. I was young and unmarried (except to the market), so at that point it made more sense to take a risk and try my hand at something completely different.

> **Bayesian Statistics**
>
> A subset of the field of statistics in which the evidence about the true state of the world is expressed in terms of degrees of belief or, more specifically, Bayesian probabilities.

In this way, I was starting from scratch. So it's important to step back for a bit and review the process of how it is that we learn to become experts.

We've discussed a lot of the nuts and bolts of how to trade: establishing opening ranges, taking positions, and deciding when the odds are against you and covering. We've also discussed some extra-market research ideas within the larger context of the broad market's behavior. Those things are important, and without them, none of the following discussion will make much sense. Before we begin though, I'm going to use an analogy—that of a musician—that will help frame the purpose of this section of the book.

As a beginning musician it is important that you learn the proper technique of manipulating your instrument. If you are a drummer, it's learning how to grip the sticks; as a flutist, it's learning proper breathing techniques. Then come the fundamentals of how music is built: the scales, keys, chord structures, time, and so on. Putting those things together creates a foundation on which to build the physical skills necessary to be competent at manipulating the instrument.

There are a number of different things that have to be worked on: coordination, strength in tiny muscles you didn't know you had, and more. Months, even years, of practice and study do not make you a musician, though, because making music is not about those things. Music comes from somewhere inside us. The kinds of music we listen to affects how our brain processes it and influences the music we choose to create. Practice and listening create a buildup of knowledge about the mechanics to create an emotional response in you and then, hopefully, the person listening to you play.

Unlike music, trading isn't an art that we do for another person's pleasure, but like music our trading does communicate with other people in the market. The point of the analogy is to highlight that the same subconscious brain activity that turns a person who practices a musical instrument into a musician is the same as the activity that transforms someone who recognizes setups and market data into a trader.

For a musician, the process of getting to that state involves the repetition of writing out the keys and the chord structures, listening to intervals, and hearing how some notes work with others. There is a bit of visualization that happens, even for the most self-trained musician.

As traders, after we have spent enough time with our noses in books and been exposed to examples too numerous to count, we begin to see the patterns that emerge from the chaos of information. We can't talk about it—we're probably not even conscious of it—but we can act on it. Like the stereotype of the jazz musician who can listen to the first few bars of a song and then slide into it, adding his voice to the song seemingly without effort, but unable to reproduce it or tell you what he did and why, traders become instinctual in their understanding of the markets they trade.

So for the musician who is taking his cues from the other musicians he's playing with, after playing with a certain group of people long enough, he gets a sixth sense about what they'll do next. When he anticipates like that, he is using Bayesian probabilities to help guide his guesses. The trader who immerses himself in a market and understands its rhythms implicitly is acting similarly.

For a trader, discordant information is like a red cape for a bull. A warning bell will go off in her head and she starts to reassess the parameters under which she took the trade, when things were acting normally. If she gets a few more of those discordant bits of information, that's when it becomes actionable, and the trade feels all wrong to her.

The musician in a free-form jazz band might be hearing one member attempting to change the key of the song strange or wrong, to extend the analogy. This gut feeling of the trader that he cannot verbalize is not an intuition but rather the result of substantial, unconscious mathematical regression of old data.

Armed with new knowledge of the situation she makes her exit from the trade without remorse. If a sudden change in the market—like a reaction to a news event—contravenes her current set of expectations, then she has to let go of her accumulated knowledge and get out of the trade quickly. It is better to cut losses and ask questions later than rail in a fugue of confirmation bias that is working against the market.

The single hardest thing for traders to do is to let go of their sense of control over the market. You do not learn all there is to know only to refuse to act appropriately because you think you know more than the market. Being wrong is no fun; none of us like to be wrong. To become a successful trader means living with every mistake and moving on quickly to the next problem to solve.

For the musician, each performance has to be focused on the next note played, the next word sung. A misplayed note is in the past and is now beyond your control. Shaking it off and continuing to play is the only course of action. Every performance is an opportunity for greatness or failure. Quite a lot of the time they fail. Reviewing your performance is for after the gig, not during it. It's the same for traders; reviewing your mistakes happens after the market closes. Each bar that completes on the chart is like a well-played measure of music. It's gone and completed and it's time to look at the next bar and navigate it properly.

Elephant Walk

Reviewing your performance is a crucial bit of self-analysis. But is that enough? In my opinion, no it is not. I wish it was. Trading would be a bit easier if it was only about those things. Unfortunately, there is something else that needs to be considered and internalized: the identification and disposition of the biggest players in the market. Not only is this important, I believe it's the most important factor in moving markets.

In the same way that the migration behavior of elephants leaves an unmistakable trail of trampled crops and well-worn paths on the landscape, the behavior of institutional investors leaves footprints on the volume charts of the stocks they invest in. Elephants, interestingly, migrate along memorized paths that stretch over thousands of kilometers. Because of their size, they can't tread lightly through a field or a forest, so they wreak havoc on local human settlements.

> **Tip**
>
> Looking at the volume on the S&P 500 futures in the last 30 minutes of trading each day, between 3:45 and 4:15 p.m. Eastern Time, is a good indication of what the institutions are thinking about the market.

Due to their size, when institutional investors enter the market, they cannot do so all at once without wreaking havoc on the structure of bids and offers. They, instead, have to enter and exit their positions over time, buying and selling lots of stock in separate transactions. It is then incumbent upon the would-be trader to look for these elephantine footprints within volume bars to note the disposition of the institutional investors.

To do this, I like to track current trading volume with average volume. By watching the ticker and looking for footprints left on the chart, I can find clues about the current sentiment. If I'm really interested in a particular moment in a stock, I will watch a time and sales log of all the transactions and note if the large blocks of stock are trading at the ask more often than the bid or vice versa. Again, we're now looking at market delta and the footprints that institutional investors leave in their wake. This is particularly helpful when a stock is approaching a breakout from a range.

Institutional traders will engage in buying and selling patterns that will become unmistakable through time and observation. You will see them trampling through the chart on the bid or the ask but trying to tiptoe while they do it.

This brings up an important point about supply and demand, which is that the equilibrium price graph put up on the blackboard of any Economics 101 class is a fiction. Why this is important will take a bit to explain. Like chemical equilibrium, economic equilibrium exists only in theory. In the physical world, true equilibrium of matter can exist only in the absence of energy, at absolute zero.

Even an object like a glass jar, which to the naked eye looks like it is unchanging, is still a seething mass of collisions of atoms, bonds being broken and reformed continually, as the external force of background heat in your kitchen and the earth's gravity act upon it. The amount of background energy in the room is not enough to change the jar for our uses at room temperature, but heat it up and it will eventually melt; if you act on it with an extreme force, it will change. Conversely, leave a glass bottle sitting on your counter for 100 years and it will sag, because glass is a liquid that is moving extremely slowly, so slowly that it gives the appearance of being a solid object.

Equilibrium, therefore, is something one can only perceive in a time-relative sense; it is a condition that can be approached but not fully reached when all things acting in a system are considered. It is governed by Zeno's Paradox. Markets vibrate back and forth, much like electrons and atoms, except that instead of measuring energy transfers between collisions, we are measuring price. The forces that act upon a market are many and varied: interest rate shifts, infrastructure failure, weather, exchange rate fluctuations, and so on. Institutions react to these forces differently than individuals.

Information in a market is not perfect. It does not move instantaneously, even though the Internet moves at the speed of light to disseminate it. This time lag creates volatility in pricing as markets react clumsily to new inputs. Moreover, the biggest players in the market hold sway over the application of the new information based on their conclusions, no matter how wrong they may be. The shorter your time frame for trading markets, the more closely you are at the whim of what the big boys are doing because they can wield their money like a weapon. If they, like the elephant, cannot or will not change their behavior, it does not matter what information you may have that leads you to different conclusions about a stock's price, the market will continue slowly reacting to the new data.

Therefore, it is important to live in the moment to glean what those big boys are doing, but it's also important to put that in the context of the bigger picture of the market. For example, is this a bullish move up near the top of a consolidation range in a longer-term bear market? If so, then you can calculate the probability of a reversal from that time perspective and act accordingly.

Moves that happen with strong momentum do not flame out in a few bars; they push through the short-term volatility and run, while moves made without conviction tend to flame out and reverse without much fanfare.

Breadth of a market move is also an important footprint left by institutions. For example, the Dow Jones is weighted by price rather than capitalization, so a few companies can make it or break it. A few blue chip stocks can mask the actual supply and demand for stocks. Tracking the ratio of gainers to losers will also help guide your bias towards your trades giving you a holistic view of where the big money is going and why.

Breakouts versus Reversals

The disposition of the heavy hitters in the market influences how the market trades. The length and breadth of consolidation and trending waves are wholly dependent on where they are placing their capital as net buyers or sellers. Taking your trading cues from them will improve your decision making in whatever type of trade you put on. There really are only two types of trades:

1. The breakout trade
2. The reversal trade

Everything else is noise. We've discussed all of these trades at various points so far in the book, but not in any rigorous way. Let's take them now in order.

The first one happens after an established range has been violated either up or down; the market is changing from a consolidation state to a trending state. The breakout move will continue as long as the supply of buyers can lift the bids of sellers. Buying comes in two flavors, new longs that see the price as a bargain and old shorts that are now exiting, buying to cover.

Looking at short interest as a percentage of the total float (shares outstanding for purchase) is a good clue for assessing the violence of breakouts. Total short interest (in number of shares) versus average daily volume tells you how long it would take for all the shorts to cover their positions. For example, if a stock has 10 million shares sold short and the average volume is 500,000 shares traded per day, it will take a minimum of

20 days of normal trading to clear all of those short positions. If the price begins to move up and the shorts begin to cover, that creates upward energy on the price of the stock, as they have to lift offers to buy back that which they sold short.

The combination of new longs acting on news and fundamentals with a massive number of shares sold short creates potentially explosive buying pressure. Knowing the disposition of the market and the context of what may be a routine opening-range breakout could be the difference between a trade paying you modestly and making you a small fortune. Use the volume delta to tell you if there are still buyers coming in to lift offers even though statistics may indicate that the probability of the stock going higher is against you. At that point, once the volume delta slows down, it is time to get out of the trade, as the supply of buyers will soon be overwhelmed by sellers who think the price has risen too far too fast.

The breakout trade that moves higher on volume and remains high has the potential of trapping new short sellers that piled into the breakout and are then forced to continually cover at higher prices, incurring small losses each time.

The reversal trade is, in a sense, the complete opposite of the breakout trade. It looks for exhaustion of a trending move and establishes a position against it. This type of trade is looking for mean reversion, acting on the premise that the current trend has overshot fair value enough to make it worth establishing a position. The more violent the move that you are looking to trade against, the more likely the trade will be at least minimally profitable. Any move that is parabolic in shape will eventually reach a tipping point where no new fresh buyers or sellers can be found at that price. In the short term, the price is unsustainable regardless of the fundamentals of the stock.

Reversals from parabolic extremes are very low-risk trades because of the mania that they imply on one side of the market—greed for the rising market and fear in the falling one. Markets that are trending at an increasing rate over shorter and shorter time frames carry with them a high probability of profit from a reversal once volume is incapable of pushing the price any farther.

Lastly, I want to make a point about looking at the activity of the bid versus asking prices. Changes in the behavior at that margin are helpful in detecting shifts in sentiment and spotting potential reversals.

Ultimately, it is the amount of buying or selling pressure in a short time period that overwhelms the current array of bids and offers that creates movement. Large blocks trading hands intermittently will not have an influence on price.

Losing Your Inhibitions

It is now time to look at the factors that inhibit a person from becoming an expert trader. In my experience there are two that dominate, overshadowing the others and causing the lion's share of the mistakes that aspiring traders make. One is tied to the mismatch of time frame and attention, and the other is a lack of discretion in filtering out the noise of the markets.

As we discussed previously, the process of building up implicit knowledge about how a market trades is important. You cannot build up the necessary intimacy with the ebbs and flows of the market without that information being streamed into your brain, allowing your subconscious to process and organize the data into trading actions without being paralyzed by faulty pattern recognition and information overload.

The person who studies markets without prioritizing a few specific patterns that emerge runs the very real risk of internalizing none of them. The result is *paralysis by analysis*, which happens when the brain cannot distinguish one pattern from the next. Worse, it can't make a decision on what the patterns mean, and therefore cannot take decisive and precise action, but rather diddles around trying to rationalize why it is that he sits and watches his profit leak away or his losses pile up.

A high level of cognitive focus is needed for implicit learning. Jumping from chart to chart looking for correlations or confirmations creates what researchers call *interference effects*, which are simply the results of excess information—gathered before or after pattern recognition—that interferes with the processing and internalizing of the pattern. Information overload is a real problem for the diligent and enthusiastic person.

There are some people with highly trained and active minds that can process a staggering amount of information. If you listen to them speak about their work, they can dazzle you with the breadth of their knowledge and ability to draw parallels between markets. Their skill in synthesizing and reducing the markets to digestible nuggets of information can be equally impressive. But ask them how successful they are at translating that knowledge into trading profits and that same impressive command of the markets will create a picture of a conflicted and paralyzed person, unable to use the prodigious amount of information at their fingertips to do anything other than comment on the market.

These people become trapped in a vicious cycle, thinking that every trade has to be made within the context of all known information, as opposed to forcing that to the side and concentrating on the task at hand. Trading is hard enough to do without being your own worst enemy. All of that information is important, but before and after the trade only. During the trade, your only focus should be whether the next bar will go up or down and by approximately how much.

So while I keep advocating study, research, and review, you can have too much of a good thing. The lesson is to master a few tradable patterns. Once you are familiar with them, you can then be comfortable in making decisions without fear of being wrong. Not every trade works out, no matter how well you think it through because nothing can remove the uncertainty from the markets.

Markets are not predictable; they are probabilistic.

Markets are ruled by hearts and minds, not just minds. And those hearts and minds are full of conflicting, erroneous, and outdated information. If you can strip out as much of that information from your trading as possible then you can and will be successful. That is the advantage the professional trader has over the amateur.

In short, it is less important to master the understanding of indicators and charts patterns and more important to observe and internalize them through time.

I learned this lesson so well that when I went back into the market in late 2003–04, as I said before, I did very well. Having applied the principles and distilled them down to what I needed and like a great jazz musician was so in tune with the markets that I was able to trade very successfully. As I said before, it became routine and almost boring.

We acquire money to be able to afford to do the things in life we wish to do, whatever they may be. At the end of 2007, I found myself in a very interesting place, one where I had succeeded almost beyond what I thought possible, but I was restless, as there was little challenge in my life. My success created the added benefit of reconciling with my parents. While they still did not understand why I would want to live such an unpredictable life, they came to respect my desire to do so.

It was in late 2007 that I became fascinated with the idea of working in a frontier market. This presented a completely different kind of challenge than that of learning how to trade in very well established markets like those in Toronto and New York. Say what you want about Wall Street and Bay Street, but their markets operate on a specific set of rules and principles. If you want to play in those markets, you have to learn the rules, whether you agree with them or not. This book is not about the current political climate in which Wall Street operates. That is not germane to the subject at hand and did not guide my decision to strike out into the financial wilderness of Vietnam.

I picked Vietnam for a couple of reasons: first and foremost, because it was, in 2007, the second fastest growing economy in the world; and second, because I am of Vietnamese decent. I decided to apply myself to the building of a financial information infrastructure, which was wholly nonexistent in Vietnam. I saw this as an opportunity, not only to challenge myself, but also to help the people of my homeland find a more prominent and profitable place in the world economy. As the saying goes, a rising tide lifts all boats. With those things in mind, I set forth on a different kind of journey, full of the same kind of enthusiasm and naiveté that marked my initial foray into the capital markets.

I headed out to Vietnam to invest my accumulated wealth in building a financial media infrastructure, which I felt the country was sorely lacking. To do this I stopped trading and focused my energies on building that enterprise. I left my investments on autopilot and became one of those people who, when removed from their comfort zone and the context in which they learned how to trade, lose their edge and can't trade successfully. I stopped utilizing my own trading rules, though at the time I did not realize it. Compounding this loss of focus on trading was the brewing financial crisis that was emerging in the U.S. housing market, the so-called subprime crisis. The combination of those things, plus the inherent risk associated with venture startups, created a toxic financial potion.

In short, I went broke again.

Reversal of Fortune

I thought my first experience with an event like this would have prepared me for it emotionally. It didn't. There was no comparison, frankly. I was devastated, not only for myself but for my parents as well. I had convinced them to trust me with some of their money, and in my arrogance I, of course, lost that as well.

My mistakes began, like everything else, by doing too much. Not only did I bite off well more than I could chew, but I also didn't realize I had done so until it was far too late. Trying to build a financial media company for a market that wasn't ready for it while the entire financial world was melting down around me was a recipe for disaster. When I think back on it now, I wonder just what made me think I could do that and not fail completely.

Mine was a juggling act where I threw the balls into the air and missed them coming back down. They'd hit the ground and shattered and I was still looking up waiting for them to return.

Since I was trying to build a business, I had staff to manage, payroll to meet, and all of the 1,001 little decisions that have to be made to make a financial startup work. Anyone who has started a business from scratch knows that it's an all-consuming process. It has to be if you want it to be anything close to successful. Businesses take time and require nurturing. Do you think I was keeping a weather eye on the markets? Do you think I was applying any of the ideas and concepts that I'd learned so well while working in New York and Toronto? Do you think I was listening to the market as it went through one of the worst periods in its history?

No. Of course not.

I became one of those guys I talked about earlier. Removed from the context that made me a good trader—the place where I learned my craft—I thought I was making smart and informed choices, but I wasn't. Worse than that, as the pressure mounted, my decisions became more and more desperate. I took on more risk that I could not manage, convinced that what was happening was not happening to me. Meanwhile, the business was falling apart, payroll was not being met. My friends whom I'd drafted into this venture left and in the end I lay down in my bed one Saturday evening and realized that I had no idea where my next month's rent was going to come from.

Here I was, in a third world country, with no friends, no job, no money, and, at this point, no one to help me. I'm not writing this to ask for your pity. I bring it up because it is important to remember that no matter who you think you are or what you think you are capable of, we all have our limits.

Markets are treacherous. They are designed to part you from your money and your time. You are not special. None of us are charmed. All of the things that my hard work and good intentions had brought me turned to ash in a few short months. And I literally had nothing to show for it.

I spent 2008 and most of 2009 in a place I had never been before, living day to day and wondering how I was going to keep a roof over my head and food in my stomach. It was worse than when I'd set out on my own and lived on Andrew's couch. At least then I had a job and some support system around me, but during this time I didn't have any fallback position. I'd alienated nearly everyone in my life through my arrogance and pride.

Did I deserve what I got handed to me? I don't know. Certainly I have no one to blame other than myself, and I wouldn't dare to consider avoiding that responsibility. To me, I believe that as, Clint Eastwood's character said at the end of the great movie *Unforgiven*, "Deserve's got nothin' to do with it."

I can say that now, but I certainly was not saying it to myself at the time.

Some people say that luck is where preparation meets opportunity; others believe in divine providence. I just know that sometimes breaks come your way. Anhtoan was one of my breaks.

His assistance was invaluable. A venture capitalist, among other things, Anhtoan saw enough in me to give me some work—freelance content creation and research mostly—to keep me from completely drowning. I was able to scrape together enough money to live, if just barely. If you've ever been in this situation, you know how tough your decisions are. You are forced to ask, "Do I pay the electric bill or eat lunch this week?" More important, you learn to live with that level of uncertainty. It becomes, in many ways, your entire world. It lives with you like a homunculus on your shoulder, and it eventually becomes its own form of sickness.

Those who live with chronic physical pain compensate for it by altering their movements to avoid the pain. This causes a cascade of problems, where neck pain leads to shoulder pain, which pulls on the hip that pulls on the knee. Managing the pain itself becomes an illness, inflicting stress. Emotional pain, unfortunately, is no different.

I once had enough money to live comfortably on for the rest of my life, and it was devastating to remember that as I made subsistence-level decisions. In many ways, I will never fully recover from it.

The full magnitude of my mistake, though, did not sink in until my grandmother died. I hadn't really hit rock bottom until then. First, I had to ask Anhtoan for the cab fare to just get to the funeral, and then, because my parents could not come over from Canada in time, I had to represent the family during a Buddhist funeral. For those who do not know, this entails nearly a week of putting affairs in order, prayer, ceremony, and grieving. I remember feeling so completely inadequate that it overwhelmed me.

I was living on borrowed cab fare and time, and I brought that and pretty much nothing else to honor my grandmother's life and memory. I can safely say she deserved better than that.

Of course, in my grief and self-pity I was forgetting everything that I had done right. While reviewing your mistakes can be cathartic, it can also be poisonous if you do not accept them, put them behind you, and forgive yourself, if only a little bit. And forgiving yourself is one of the hardest things to do. It is a simple thing, but it is also the gulf between success and failure.

When I think back on this period of my life, I'm amazed at the little things that seemed so important at the time. When you have nothing, any threat to what little you have is magnified. It is sad to say, but during those early days I had to scratch for the littlest of scraps. One thing that makes Vietnam so attractive in today's global economy is the availability of cheap labor, both skilled and unskilled. And guess what? I had become part of that labor force. The Peter of the past, who was used to maintaining a lifestyle shuttling between Toronto and New York, had disappeared. I was just a guy working for people who knew less about the business than I did and I had to accept it, because ten bucks is better than nothing.

As painful as that period was, it was also instructive. One doesn't go through something like that and take anything for granted anymore.

Again, while some believe in fate or luck or karma, all I know is that the universe forgave me a little bit because right after I got home from the funeral, my phone rang.

What I'd forgotten was that, while I had no monetary capital, I did have considerable human capital: friends, contacts, and associates that I had made, who, when the time was right, would be a resource for me. The phone call was from a contact that was putting together a research team at a local investment house. It was not much of a job, but it was a start. And with that start came my rebirth. While it was very difficult to pull off and required an even deeper swallowing of my pride, I am very grateful that it has carried me through to today.

The adversity I suffered fundamentally altered my perspective on trading, further distilling it down to almost obvious simplicity. I came to see the markets only in terms of reversals.

Markets are ultimately psychological phenomena. The price discovery mechanism does not always seem rational to the outside observer, who is not caught up in the emotional roller coaster of the greed-versus-fear dichotomy. Embedded in all of our discussions so far has been this idea when markets act emotionally, they tend to overdo it to one extreme or another.

People act in their own self-interest in very predictable ways, but like all informational systems, if the data they receive has errors in it, they will still act as though the information were correct. Like objects governed by Newton's First Law of Motion, people will continue making financial decisions until their understanding of the data change. When the illusion can no longer be maintained, a loss of confidence in the current pricing structure quickly reverses and the bubble created by the dislocation corrects itself.

The important point here is to understand that these distortions or dislocations, illusory as they may be, can go on for a very long time. They create the reality we are living in and can last beyond what any adept or forward-thinking person can believe is possible. In the same way that P.T. Barnum said that no man ever went broke underestimating the vulgarity of the American public, markets can continue in a trend far longer than the fundamentals of the market imply.

To venture back toward psychology, which is where markets ultimately play, the mass psychology of buying begets more buying (likewise selling begets more selling), until an outside force acts with sufficient force so as to change the behavior in the aggregate.

So knowing this, how can we utilize it to assess the probabilities of when and how reversals in market sentiment will come about? What are the signals, warning bells?

There is a distribution of people of varying skill, attention, and risk tolerance arrayed across time horizons as short as milliseconds (thanks to high-frequency trading [HFT] computer algorithms) to weeks (long-term buy-and-hold investors). When you stop and look at it, there are millions of variables to consider, all changing in real time.

But because human behavior is predictable and purposeful—only people's priorities are unknowable—the one thing is constant is the shape of the distribution of changes in price over all of the time horizons. The size of the price change may be radically different, but the distribution of the price changes is the same as one pulls out from the second-to-second to the day-to-day time frame.

Let's move from the abstract to the concrete to illustrate my point. During a particular trading day, there is an opening-range breakout that is common in markets. They happen all the time. Relative to that time frame, say 15 minutes, the opening-range breakout that occurs is extreme. It's relatively enormous. Pulling back to look at an entire week's worth of trading, that opening-range breakout is now uninteresting. Those who are watching the one-minute ticker are responding to extreme

Table 4.1 Average Range Stats for AAPL

Time	Average Range
Daily	$0.64
Weekly	$1.60
Monthly	$4.11

changes in price predictably, and will buy or sell aggressively based on their bias.

Harkening back to our statistics from Chapter 3, Table 4.1 has the average ranges for Apple (AAPL) from daily to monthly. To a day-trader, an $0.80 move would be considered abnormal, especially if it happened in 30 minutes, but to a swing trader or someone looking at markets from a weekly basis, $0.80 may be a move that he would begin considering trading off of. Meanwhile, the long-term investor looking at the monthly chart would very likely consider such a move to be noise.

The same is true for traders focused on price changes that occur on an hourly basis. They ignore the minute-to-minute wiggles in price and do not act until the chart looks extreme, possibly showing the deviation as something to sell into. Once that happens they enter the market. In this way traders focused on larger time periods become the catalysts for reversals in price.

This brings up one of the very real dangers of HFT, which now, by some estimates, makes up more than 70 percent of all volume on the exchanges. If most of the market is focused on the millisecond time frame, then there are fewer participants focused further out to provide a rational brake for extremes of sentiment. It should follow then that markets have become more and more volatile because of the preponderance of this style of trading. In other words, directional moves with this kind of non-normal (in a statistical sense) distribution of capital arrayed along the various time horizons become even more exaggerated than they would under a normal distribution.

Like objects in motion, markets tend to stay in motion until otherwise impacted; and markets without natural brakes will move towards ever more dangerous extremes. This makes markets much more unpredictable and treacherous. Bubbles are created when everyone along all time horizons is getting the same signal, and prices move in an exponential manner when everyone is crowded on one side of the market. The reversal there happens only when there is no one left to bid the price higher. It's similar to breakout exhaustion, but in the most extreme sense.

One cannot discount margin-related selling from this analysis, either. In all extreme market moves, someone on the short or long side of the market is getting forced out at the margin. Momentum traders will keep adding to their positions as long as the margin-related selling continues. At some point it is not psychology but rather the stability and solvency of the brokerages and clearinghouses that determines the outcome, which is why they grant themselves that protection in their margin agreement with clients. If you trade on margin, and anyone selling short is by definition on margin, you must factor that into your thinking as a momentum or breakout trader.

The reversal trader is waiting for the opportunity to pounce after the margin calls and panic subside. Once the bargain hunters focused on the long term come in, they start buying with both fists. No tentative, toe-in-the-water behavior here, but a statement big enough to absorb the panic and arrest it. Buyers have to be large enough and committed enough to do this or the selling will not abate.

Market corrections attempt to restore rational valuations. And since the bubble or previous trend created a wealth of opportunity on the way up that was somewhat illusory, the bursting of that illusion, like exposing the Wizard behind the curtain, will be of equal size, but not time. Thus, when illusions fail they do not happen gradually, like the buildup to the peak, they happen all at once as everyone comes to the same conclusion at the same time. Momentum that was the perma-bulls' friend on the way up now becomes their enemy on the way down.

Once all the above factors are in full flight, the market will continue to drop until it arrests itself. Obvious technical support levels will be the first places tested, but as we know, they hold no predictive value. There is no prize for calling a bottom other than the pride of doing so. The market is not about pride; it is about finding the arbitrage between the current price and potential future price and exploiting it. Buying into a falling market or shorting a runaway uptrend is a good way to lose a lot of money in a hurry.

A good example of when something looked like an extreme market drop but did not turn out to be a bottom was the time in September 2001 after the 9/11 tragedy. There was not a sufficient concentration of volume and price changes on the down side of the market to produce a definitive bottom after the bursting of the dot-com bubble that began in August of 2000 on the S&P 500 Index. The market did not bottom until a year later in October of 2002.

Traders Do It with Frequency

No discussion of modern trading techniques can be complete without at least mentioning the effects of high-frequency, computer-generated trading. Estimates are that by 2010 nearly 70 percent of all trades taking place were of this type. In other words, humans behind screens make up less than 30 percent of all trading activity in Western markets. The goals of the HFT platform and an algorithmic approach to trading is to essentially be microscopic scalpers, working sometimes in the fractions of a second with large volume to pull a profit off the market measured in fractions of a cent per share.

In our previous discussion about identifying the disposition of institutional investors—the big boys in the market—I was alluding to this influence. HFT exists in all markets: stocks, bonds, options, futures, and so on. The advantage for the hedge fund or investment bank's trading division is that, theoretically, the risk-to-variability ratio for an HFT approach can be much higher than for more traditional forms of trading and investing.

This kind of trading is not available to you or me, as the Securities and Exchange Commission (SEC) and Financial Industry Regulatory Authority (FINRA) have regulations for us to contend with, and broker's fees would far exceed any profit we could eke out, anyway. The dominance of HFT algorithms has changed the tenor of the market over the past twelve years that I've been trading, but it is ultimately just another factor that needs to be internalized to help guide your decisions. It is a verity of the modern marketplace and you need to be aware of its effects.

Rules of Engagement

This chapter has covered a lot of ground, providing you with a perspective on time and your decisions within the time frame you devote to trading. That means it's *time* (all pun intended) to put it all together and present some rules to follow.

There are essentially two different conditions happening in a market at all times:

1. The price is breaking to a new high or low.
2. The price is reversing from a new high or low.

It sounds almost pedantic to say that, but it is the truth. Even range-bound markets are making new highs and lows. They are happening within shorter time frames than the one you are currently looking at, but they are still happening. Defining market behavior this way then implies the following two statements:

1. If the price is NOT making a new high, then it must be reversing from the high.
2. If the price is NOT making a new low, then it must be reversing from the low.

The best trading opportunities occur just after a new high or low has been made. The more the price moves away from the previous day's high or low, the greater the probability that a reversal of some magnitude will happen. There is no hard and fast rule for the magnitude of a reversal; just that it will happen.

I've found that applying a reversal strategy commonly used in foreign currency exchange trading also works well in equity trading, with a few small modifications. I'm going to discuss this only in terms of a long side reversal trade (i.e., identifying the trend low and buying stock to ride the reversal higher).

After a breakdown of the opening range we would expect longs to liquidate and short sellers to pile on, pushing the stock down quickly, away from the support level. As the trend moves away from that price, volume will accelerate as long as sellers outnumber buyers and the price continues to move down. As volume begins to slow and the price reaches a level where the supply of sellers better matches the supply of buyers, the opportunity for a reversal arises.

While watching the ticker on a move down, there tends to be a series of bars where the volume reaches a crescendo and the supply of sellers is met with an equal number of buyers. Once that happens there will be a period where the volume will dry up and volume deltas will become very small, a sure sign that sellers have left the market. At that point you can begin looking for a reversal bar, the criteria for which is an opening price above the opening price of the previous down day. This is a high-percentage setup because the stock is in a bullish posture and if the range between the open and the previous high is low, then that makes for a small opening range, with the possibility, on a break, of seeing a large move that day.

Let's again look at AAPL again, but this time we'll use some more recent data. The stock had been in a multiple-week downtrend that culminated on June 28, 2012 (Figure 4.1). The volume on June 26 through 28 was the lightest it had been in weeks, less than half of the volume in May. So this was a good sign that sellers had all but abandoned the stock. On Friday,

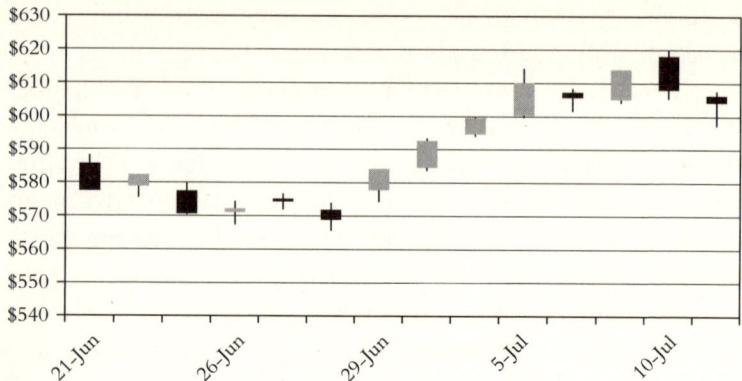

Figure 4.1 Gap Open Reversal Example (AAPL Daily Chart June–July 2012)

Table 4.2 Data for Gap Open Reversal

Date	Open	High	Low	Close	Volume
6/27/2012	575	576.74	571.92	574.5	7249900
6/28/2012	571.67	574	565.61	569.05	10101300
6/29/2012	578	584	574.25	584	15033500
7/2/2012	584.73	593.47	583.6	592.52	14269800
7/3/2012	594.88	600	594	599.41	8619500
7/5/2012	600.56	614.34	599.65	609.94	17287900
7/6/2012	607.09	608.44	601.58	605.88	14961800
7/9/2012	605.3	613.9	604.11	613.89	13534200

June 29, AAPL opened above not only the previous open but also the previous high, which made it an outside day at the open (Table 4.2).

The average daily range for AAPL over the past year was $9.91. If there were going to be a reversal, it would have gone no farther than the previous low, $565.61, and much more probably to the previous high, $574. AAPL opened at $578, dipped to $574.25, and closed at $584. When it opened at $578, setting an opening range of −$0.25 and asking what the probability was that it would drop $4.00 to $574, the previous high, would have yielded 52.7 percent.

Apple reached a low of $574.25 and closed the day at $584. Since the $574 support held, it was a good bet that the stock would fully reverse and continue higher since it had only moved $3.75 and the total range for the day should have been almost $10. So once Apple crossed $578.25, there was an opportunity to buy with confidence that it would not be selling off that day. This was a bullish reversal setup that gapped up on the open, retested previous support, and then rallied higher.

If you were trading this on a daily basis, you would wait for the stock to close after such a bullish open and take a position on Monday because of the importance of Fridays, discussed in Chapter 2.

If you had wanted to play it intraday based on the setup, that was possible as well by taking a position once the price was safely back over the opening price and grabbing a few extra bucks for your troubles.

A more conservative reversal strategy is the *two-bar reversal*, which is one where, after a downtrend plays itself out, the reversal up bar occurs and you wait to take a position until after the second up bar closes above the high of the first reversal bar. The example in Figure 4.1 is an extreme reversal pattern, the *gap up*, where the reversal bar opened above the previous down bar. Stocks with extremely bullish charts and statistic sets will exhibit this behavior. For AAPL from July 2011 to July 2012, it would break the previous daily high 59.1 percent of the time, while it would only break the previous low 33.3 percent of the time. This tells you that, on balance, AAPL has more buyers coming into it than sellers day to day.

The criteria for going long is as follows: After two consecutive uptick (reversal) bars, if the price exceeds the high of the second reversal bar, go long at that price, just above the second reversal day's high—say 0.1 percent above that price (your opening range for this trade). Set your stop at the low first reversal bar. Appendix C has a method for setting up the test in a spreadsheet.

This strategy gives you a high percentage entry point, which minimizes the probability of the trade going bad while taking advantage of extremes in sentiment that tend to reverse to the mean. I've computed the data for the S&P 500 over the last 12 years and, given these criteria, this type of setup is profitable 64 percent of the time for long reversals (i.e., the price went higher without violating your stop 64 percent of the time). That's a great edge. It's better than getting dealt a pair of aces in Texas Hold'em.

Turn Around and Make Money

Let's look a little more closely at the two-bar reversal strategy and make sure that it's clear how the setup works. We're going to shift off of AAPL and look at a different stock, one of their suppliers, Nvidia (NVDA). Early in 2012 NVDA put in a textbook two-bar reversal pattern that was potentially very lucrative.

After the turn of the New Year, NVDA went on a small rally but it stalled and the stock sold off during the week of January 9. This culminated with a big down bar on January 17, when the stock hit a low of $13.50, as shown in Figure 4.2 and Table 4.3. January 17 was a Monday, bringing a high probability that, given a reversal on Tuesday, Monday's low would be the low for the week. The range on the 17th was $0.44, and

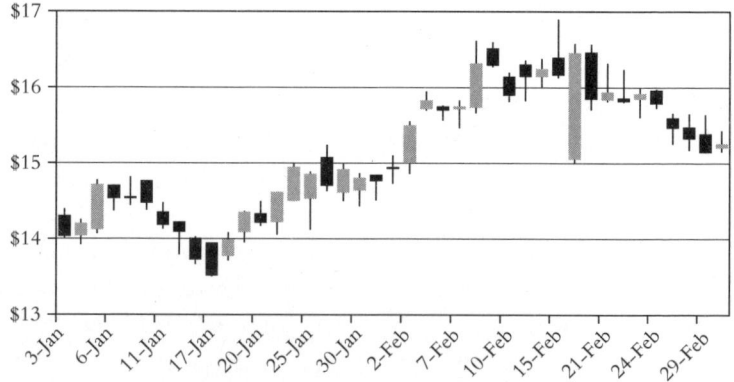

Figure 4.2   Two-Bar Reversal Chart, NVDA (2012)

Table 4.3 Open-High-Low-Close (OHLC) Data for Figure

Date	Open	High	Low	Close	Volume
1/13	14	14.03	13.66	13.73	12,607,500.00
1/17	13.94	13.94	13.5	13.52	15,679,400.00
1/18	13.78	14.09	13.71	13.98	15,816,900.00
1/19	14.1	14.37	13.95	14.35	15,207,800.00
1/20	14.33	14.5	14.17	14.22	13,656,800.00
1/23	14.23	14.62	14.05	14.61	14,069,800.00
1/24	14.51	15	14.5	14.94	18,200,600.00

the average daily range for NVDA over the past year was a very high $0.76 (data not shown), especially for a $12–15 stock. NVDA opened on January 18 at $13.78, above the close on the 17th and within $0.16 of the previous high. The probability of reversing the old downtrend was 61.7 percent.

When that happened and the stock closed up for the day, it was the first bar of a potential reversal pattern, but one bar does not a pattern make. Two consecutive closes in the opposite direction of the previous trend is a far stronger position than just one bar, creating a 64 percent chance of going higher without violating the previous trend's low. Also working in our favor is the close above the previous day's open and high price.

On the 19th, the situation is looking good for a potential reversal trade. So far the range for the week has been $0.59, which is very small versus the average weekly range of $1.54. The stock is not overextended in that sense. NVDA closed within $0.13 of the high for the week so far. Having risen $0.04 over the weekly open, the probability that it will rise another $0.10 to best the previous day's high is 75.2 percent for the 19th and 89.2 percent for any day for the rest of the week. The odds are looking good that the second reversal bar will arrive.

And it does. The 19th opens at $14.10, $0.01 above the high on the 18th, creating a high break on the open, which gives us a very good chance for a two-bar reversal because the odds of the open being the high for the day are just 2.4 percent per the data from the past year (see the supporting data in Appendix D).

Now that two up bars have been completed in a row, it can be confirmed that the previous downtrend has been broken and a new uptrend has begun. Taking a long position at $14.38, a break of the previous day's high (Table 4.3) on January 20 would give you a 50.6 percent chance to see the stock move $0.56 before Friday's close. (The stock had moved $0.44 above the open, so the probability is 50.6 percent that it would move $1.00.) The average range for the week is $1.54, and so far the stock has traded within a $0.88 range, so the probabilities are good that there's more to this rally this week.

Analyzing this setup this way is very conservative. A trader who was working with hourly or 30-minute data would have captured more of the reversal because the moves were so big. A less dramatic reversal would have been where the price did not exceed the last down bar until sometime during the second reversal bar. In Figure 4.3, I've altered the NVDA data to show the difference.

The data for January 18–20 has been altered to detail a more normal two-bar reversal, where the first reversal bar closes within the previous bar and the second reversal bar follows through with a powerful up move, closing above the high of

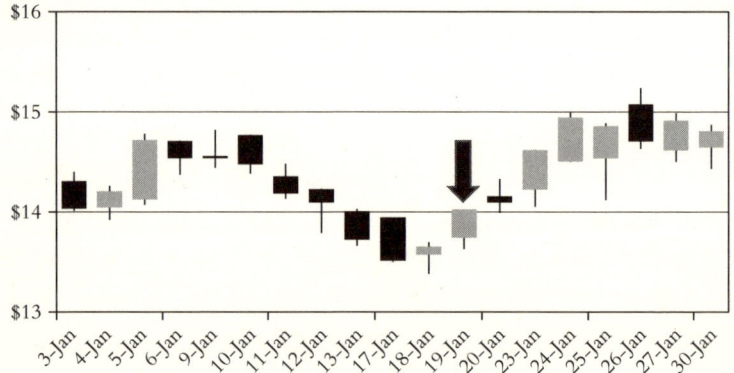

Figure 4.3 Two-Bar Reversal within Previous Down Bar (NVDA Altered History 2012)

the last down bar in the previous trend. That is a very important level of resistance, and a close above that price is significant. Once you've been through that, on the next day you can take a position with confidence that the previous trend has been arrested and a trade is possible.

Heading for the Exits

There are a number of methods I've found that work well to time my exit from a trade. Buying is easier than selling for most people. My hope here is to give you tools that will make both decisions equally easy for you. I've shown you how to assess the strength of a setup, so it's up to you to tailor that knowledge to the type of setups you'll take positions on and what time frame you'll trade in. I can't tell you what the best situation for you will be; I can only show you how to do it, then encourage you to find what makes you the most money.

The first exit strategy is really easy; it's the two-bar reversal in reverse. Simply, exiting the trade means waiting for two down bars to complete and covering at the opening of the third (Figure 4.4). Like conservatively waiting until two bars

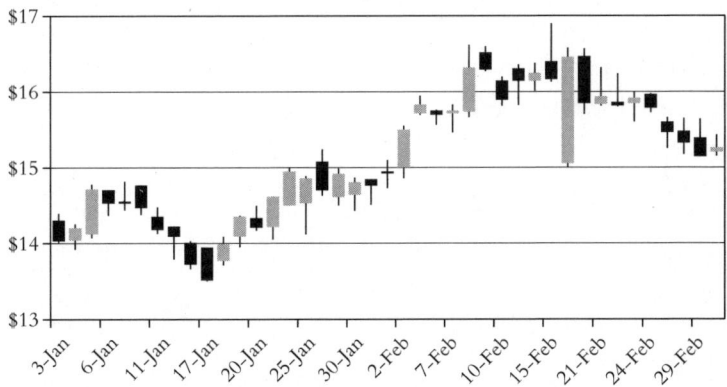

Figure 4.4 NVDA Two-Bar Reversal Chart (2012)

complete before initiating a position, staying conservative and waiting until the second bar completes makes selling mechanical and stress free.

Going back to our NVDA example and looking at the full chart again, we see that the trade would have stayed on for a few weeks, as there was no instance where NVDA closed lower than it opened two days in a row until February 10. To recall, in our example, we initiated a position at $14.38 on January 20. NVDA closed on February 10 at $15.90 per share, a gain of $1.52 per share or 10.6 percent. Since February 10 was a Friday and the odds were very good coming into the close that the stock would close down, covering the position before the close of the week would have been prudent, once the probability was good that it would be a down bar. Your probabilities work for you when you go to sell as much as they do when you go to buy. As you practice trading this way, these things will become more obvious. Looking at the probabilities for this exit, Table 4.4 holds some clues.

On February 8 NVDA bolted up to $16.62 per share and settled back to $16.30 on the close. Volume was very heavy—three times what was normal. At that point the stock had exceeded both the average weekly and monthly price moves above the open price—$0.88 versus $0.75 on a weekly basis and $1.68 versus $1.66 on a monthly basis—so it was looking overextended. It then put in two inside days in a row, but they were both down bars and volume lightened up on both days. It turns out that there was still some life left in the rally but the easy money was made by closing the position on February 10 after the

Table 4.4 Statistics at the Beginning of the Reversal Bar

	Weekly	Monthly
Range	$1.16	$1.89
Average Range	$1.54	$3.50
High − Open	$0.88	$1.68
Average + Open	$0.75	$1.66

second closing bar. The extreme volatility that ensued after that was not worth trading. Executing your trades is difficult enough on normal or boring days, trying to trade when the market is going haywire because of news or some major announcement, like a Federal Reserve statement, is not worth the risk.

For this two-bar reversal setup and a stock as volatile as NVDA, trading it on only a daily basis is not the optimal path to making money. You may make more money refining reversals in the hourly or 30-minute time frames, but that does not mean that trading it with a daily focus is wrong or not recommended.

In the end, with a system like that you have to be comfortable with leaving a portion of the trending move on the table, as the great gold trader Jim Sinclair has often said, "for the God of Greed." If you feel the need to capture more of the move than the two-bar reversal strategy offers, then it may be necessary to monitor your positions intraday, creating intraday opening ranges and targets, for example hourly, to signal you during that second bar that it is time to get out before the close, and skimming off a little more profit on either end of the trade.

One of the signals in the above example that the rally may have been over was that the stock was unable to break the February 8 high on February 9, even though it opened way above the previous close. That would make me bearish on the stock for intraday trading. The absence of a break of the previous high would mean that a push above the open, if any, would be likely all the strength the stock would be able to muster that day. Now, if I'm a day-trader I'm going short the moment the stock breaks back below the opening price, using the previous day's high as a stop-loss level, in this case $16.62. The statistics for both the week and the month are telling me that the stock is overextended in those contexts, and traders who are looking at the stock on a weekly or monthly basis would be looking for an easy short after an approximately 20 percent rise in price through to peak.

Table 4.5 NVDA Data Surrounding Reversal and Short

Date	Open	High	Low	Close	Volume
2/7	$ 15.72	15.83	$ 15.46	$ 15.74	10,257,400.00
2/8	$ 15.74	$ 16.62	$ 15.66	$ 16.31	21,190,300.00
2/9	$ 16.51	$ 16.60	$ 16.27	$ 16.30	14,048,600.00
2/10	$ 16.14	$ 16.20	$ 15.81	$ 15.90	11,006,700.00
2/13	$ 16.30	$ 16.36	$ 15.82	$ 16.15	15,266,700.00
2/14	$ 16.15	$ 16.38	$ 16.01	$ 16.24	11,343,900.00
2/15	$ 16.39	$ 16.90	$ 16.13	$ 16.17	27,724,200.00
2/16	$ 15.06	$ 16.58	$ 15.00	$ 16.45	47,214,700.00

In this particular case, if you had that much profit under your belt—more than $2.00 per share at that point—covering your long and possibly going short would be a potential strategy. This would be a more aggressive strategy than the two-bar reversal strategy because there has been no confirmation via a closing price that the rally, which started in late January, was over, but the probabilities would be in your favor.

Also, going short on the February 9 close (Table 4.5) gives you a downside loss of only $0.50 per share. The close that day was $16.30, while the high on February 8 was $16.62. Setting your stop at about one percent above the high price gives you a high-probability setup for a short into the next week with very limited risk.

Looking at Figure 4.5, neither the blow off top on February 15, which saw a peak price above your stop, or the disruptive action on the 16th, when the stock opened down more than $1.00 and rallied on massive volume, did nothing to dislodge you from your short, unless you covered it near that open because neither of them closed above your stop price.

The move to $16.90 on February 15 was a low-percentage opportunity because the stock had already rallied so strongly during the month and, if it had closed above $16.80, covering the short would be necessary, but it didn't and the stock never regained that level. From there, note that there were not two up days in a row until the middle of March, where three days in a row pushed NVDA slightly higher, but it never closed

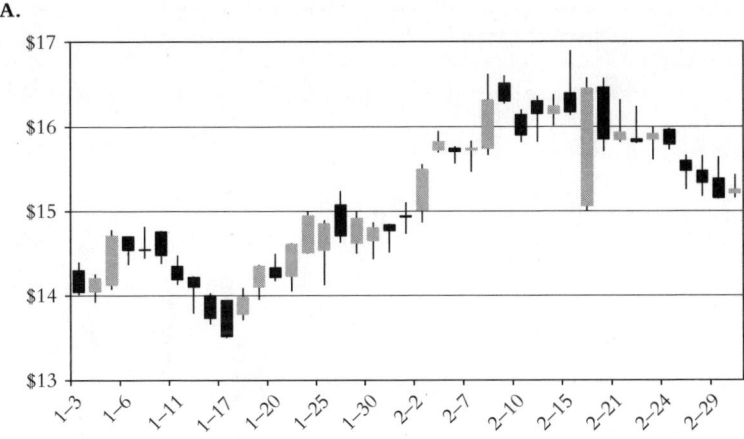

Figure 4.5 Examples of NVDA Reversal (A) and Short (B)

above $14.86, the closing price on the last down bar, shown by the arrow on Figure 4.6.

Covering on the open of the third day would have been smart. The trade was worth $1.44 or 8.8 percent. It satisfied the two-bar reversal; the range of the move for the week below the open was $0.81 versus an average move down of $0.80 (see Appendix D). But because the stock never closed above the

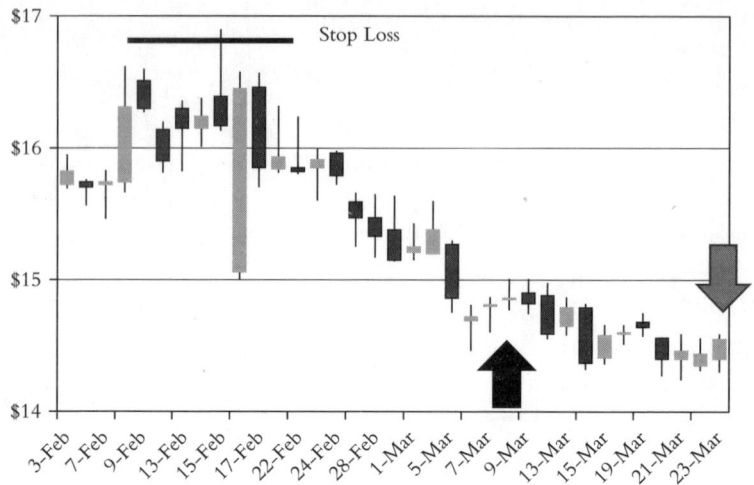

Figure 4.6 NVDA Two-Bar Reversal Short Covering

closing price of the last down bar, after three days, that acted as resistance and NVDA sold off again.

It wasn't until March 23 where the third up bar finally closed (Figure 4.6, gray arrow), on a Friday no less, at the open of the last down bar. Covering on the break of the previous closing price that day would have netted you an extra $0.41 on the trade, covering at $14.46 per share, for a gain of $1.84 or 11.3 percent.

One way to have played that interim move higher on March 6–8 was to sell off your original stake and leave the profit on the table to play with house money. If you wanted to monitor the situation closely intraday to see what was developing, that was another option. The point of the exercise was to show that while the system is designed to be as mechanical as possible, there are still moments when your judgment comes into play. It has to, as you are assessing probabilities, not making predictions. There was a solid probability that all of the money for that short position had been captured when the market closed on March 8, and walking away with nearly a 9 percent gain in less than three weeks is nothing to cry about.

Becoming a Reactionary

This approach to trading is a system built on constantly reading and reacting to new data. So as each bar develops and concludes, it is time for you to reassess your situation, recalculate your probabilities, and decide on the state of your trade or your potential to take on a position.

While trading, you are reduced to reading and reacting. Hockey coaches talk about this all the time and, as hockey is a fluid and dynamic game, it is necessary for players to become instinctual in how they make their decisions. The shorter the time frame, the more often you have to assess the state of things. Boxers work in milliseconds, so the wisdom goes, working off of micro-movements of their opponents. This is what I mean by choosing your time frame carefully as you have to learn the limits of how long it takes you to internalize all of the new information that comes with each bar and make decisions based on it. As I said, for me, breaking the market up into 30-minute segments is the sweet spot.

It's similar to what you're taught in driver's education, which is that while driving, you are constantly assessing your surroundings, working a pattern of checking your instruments and mirrors so as to know exactly where you are in relation to all other objects on the road at all times. This is the essence of defensive driving. Pilots do the same thing, routinely checking all of their instrumentation in a specific order to assess the state of the plane. Doing so greatly increases their ability to react quickly and decisively to a change in conditions that could be the difference between life and death. Time and repetition create an instinctual habit that becomes unconscious but keeps you prepared to react to potential situations before they become dangerous.

While your life is not in physical danger while trading, your money certainly is, and you want to be successful at managing your risks and preserving your capital during the process as trading becomes instinctual. This is what the jazz musician or the Formula 1 driver or any other expert goes through during the countless hours of training that provide the basis by which one can achieve great things.

I firmly believe that anyone can become great at something through desire and dedication, no matter what the activity is.

All it takes is practice and repetition; reading, reacting, and 'rithmetic.

Summary

- Watching the market is implicit learning, allowing your brain to process vast amounts of data.
  - React to discordant information quickly and decisively.
- Institutional investors leave unmistakable footprints in the volume data, so learn how to look for them.
  - Volume delta can give clues about their behavior and bias.
- There are two types of trades.
  - Breakouts and reversals.
- Implicit learning requires simplifying the types of trading one engages in.
  - Focus on the task at hand.
  - Do not juggle multiple trades.
  - Do not let your brain overthink the market.
    - The macro story is for when the market is closed.
- The market beats the best of us.
  - Especially those who do not listen to the above advice.
  - Losing everything means taking nothing for granted.
  - Markets are psychological phenomena as people try to assign value to what they perceive.
    - Emotions lead to overreactions and a mismatch of price with value.
- High frequency trading (HFT) distorts the capital structure of markets by non-normal distribution of capital arrayed versus time.

- 80+ percent of volume is now due to HFT.
  - Increased volatility and outsized momentum swings.
- Even the breakout trade is an interpretation.
  - All trades are reversal trades.
    - The price is breaking to a new high or low
    - The price is reversing from a new high or low.
- The gap-open reversal setup is an easy and very profitable one.
  - Look for opening prices close to the high or low of the previous bar.
    - This indicates a very high probability of an outside day, and therefore a breakout in that direction.
- The two-bar reversal strategy is a good conservative plan to taking a position.
  - Wait for two bars to close in the direction opposite the current trend.
  - A second reversal-bar close should be above the high of the last trending bar.
- The two-bar reversal is also a selling technique and potentially a way to immediately play the other side of the market.
  - It is somewhat conservative, but it is simple.
  - It can be combined with your other statistics to create a probability of reversal.
- This trading system is an endless series of moments where the trader reads the state of the market and reacts decisively based on the probabilities.

Chapter 5

The Range Is Your Friend

All things entail rising and falling timing. You must be able to discern this.

—*Miyamoto Musashi*

Sideways

We use the terms *bull market* and *bear market* casually, assuming that if we're not in one type of market, we must be in the other. That kind of binary "If not A, then B" logic is a very common analytic tool. It's also rarely applicable to human affairs, though it is used constantly in mass media's discussion of markets. When attempting to convey a message in easily digestible packets of information, nuance is often sacrificed and one is either a bull or a bear on whatever the topic of discussion is *du jour*. Ultimately, though, that kind of thinking is very detrimental to critical analysis of a situation. Not everything can or should be reduced to their rhetorical extremes.

If we look back over the past 100 years, we see a number of secular bull markets and only one true bear market, which would be the period of the Great Depression. The rest of the time the general market has traded in broad consolidation ranges.

It is the stated role of the central banks to mitigate the effects of a massive depression by providing countercyclical liquidity during times of credit contraction. Therefore, it is safe to assume that, given the history of the responses of the central banks since the Great Depression, it is very likely that the probability of a true bear market is rather low. In other words, their jobs are to arrest the crash by inflating the money supply in hopes of stimulating aggregate demand.

Armed with the premise that bear markets are, if not things of the past, relatively special occurrences, it makes sense to study the markets with the assumption that they have been transformed by central bank policy into longer-term, range-bound or consolidating markets.

Bull markets always end in manias, with the majority of retail investors piling in at the end during the blow-off phase of the trend. The net result is that a large swath of potential investors shies away from investing in the wake of the correction. Their capital has been devalued and there's the simultaneous recession, which is a period of debt retirement and savings rebuilding. Since the central bank will engage in countercyclical policy, the money will flow preferentially through the economy during the recovery, stimulating some sectors at different times. This is what creates consolidation in the broad market as some sectors contract or tread water and others enter mini bull markets. Understanding this dynamic, even at this basic level, will prepare you to take full advantage of a consolidating market that may last as long as 10 or 15 years.

The last such market the United States went through occurred between 1966 and 1982. It was followed by the 18-year bull market, which culminated in the dot-com bubble bursting, a whole lot of people losing their shirts (your narrator included), and the current broadly defined range-bound market we have had since then. From 2000 to the present, the U.S. stock market, as defined by the value of the S&P 500, has been in a volatile but definite range from 800 to 1550, with a dip below 800 after the failure of Lehman Brothers and the subsequent bailout of the financial system in late 2008. This supports my contention that central banks will act to prop up a market as long as they are able to do so, preferring to drive off the mal-invested capital of the boom through sideways action, over a longer period of time rather than a sharp liquidation of that same capital.

> **Alpha**
>
> The measure of the performance of a stock in relation to an index over the past year. The index is defined as having an alpha of 0.

The opportunity now exists (for the people who understand it) to use this time to accumulate stocks that will explode to the upside when the buyers re-enter the market. In a consolidating market, sellers are in greater supply, if only slightly. Even a yearlong rally will fail to breach the old high of the range because there are not enough committed buyers to overcome the sellers who see the top of the range as overpriced. The psychology of the market is, at best, neutral, but with a negative bias. The neutrality comes in the form of central bank policy, which keeps fresh buyers in the market to offset the prevailing negative sentiment while the mania of the last bull market is worked off and restructured.

Waves of Sentimentality

As I mentioned in the last section, while we have been in a relatively stagnant market for the past 10 years, there have been periods of extreme bullishness and bearishness, but not extreme enough to alter the range in the broader sense. In these times, capital that had been misallocated during previous cycles and bull markets have to be shifted and redeployed. This takes time, as the vast amount of information is digested and trends within certain sectors are eventually reversed. Those sectors that receive support through government funding tend to be the slowest to react, as they require, first, a shift in state or national political winds and, second, an overturning or modification of the legislation. These conditions create countercyclical waves within an economy: The bigger and more regulated the economy, the slower the changes will come. That said, capital is still out there trying to chase yield, and therefore it will overcompensate, rotating out of one sector and into another.

These waves within a consolidating market are not secular bull or bear markets, which mark general expansion of all sectors of the economy simultaneously. They are, rather, sector-specific bull or bear markets, which have the power to lift the value of a capitalization-weighted index but not take everyone along for the ride equally.

> ### Price-to-Earnings Ratio (P/E)
> Earnings are reported in currency per share, the same unit as the stock. A company with $1 of earnings trading at $10 per share has a P/E of 10.

By the first quarter of 2012, the average earnings on the S&P 500 was trading at a multiple of 22.8, but backing out the earnings from just two companies, Apple and Google, nearly doubled that number to 42.5. If one took out those two companies and took the next 10 companies in the index, they were trading at a P/E of 112! To say that the market at that time was top heavy would be an understatement.

Sectors move from being undervalued to being overvalued and vice versa while investors try to figure out where the best returns are. If a P/E of 15 (the long-term average of the S&P 500) was considered good for all businesses and investors deployed their capital accordingly, there would be lower—if not zero—amplitude waves in the market. It would just merrily trot along in line with GDP or the rate of monetary expansion to the tune of 5 to 6 percent per year, and books like this one would be endangered species.

But that's not how investors act. They act based on specific knowledge and specific ignorance of individual markets. Indeed, what investors don't know about a market is sometimes more important than what they do know. For example, some bank analysts have been making the argument that the core businesses of many of the major U.S. banks are not only solid but also healthy. The problem lies in the gulf between investor knowledge of this fact and the problems in those same companies' hedge books and/or trading portfolios.

When the truth of the problems finally comes to light (e.g., Lehman Brothers is a catastrophic example, as is the massive loss by J.P. Morgan's CIO office, which cost the company more than $5 billion in real earnings), the market has to react in a spastic way. What really caused me to lose my way in 2007 and 2008 was not accounting for an exponential cascade of deleveraging, which shook the entire financial world to its core. To analysts, the market is overpricing the fear of sovereign debt and litigation issues, which suppresses the share price of the entire sector.

This creates a kind of informational arbitrage that, in turn, allows investors to get overexcited both positively and negatively about certain stocks or sectors of the economy. This takes P/E levels from above average (>15) to below average (<15). The difference in the range-bound market compared to the bull market is the deviations from the long-term mean of P/E's investors are willing to accept. Expanding sectors are also offset by contracting sectors because capital is not really expanding in a low- to zero-growth environment; it is just sloshing around looking for yield. While some sectors can experience explosive growth, others necessarily have to experience lower growth or outright contraction as unprofitable firms are liquidated or absorbed because the pool of savings is not increasing.

The bull market won't start once this condition tips over a little bit. It will take all sectors expanding with pent-up demand for their stocks before the bull will be let loose. Bear markets, or even markets grinding sideways, have to prove themselves to investors. Investors become habituated to the grind and, in doing so, become inured to the hope of potential returns. They are more concerned with the return *of* their money than the return *on* their money. They demand higher standards of proof each time the high of the range is touched. They are once bitten, twice shy, as the saying goes.

This is reflected in price-to-earnings growth ratios (PEG rates). When P/Es are below average and the market is above the top of the range, it's very likely that the bull market is imminent. PEG ratios at that point should be quite high, and once the trending move occurs investors will be willing to pay a premium for growth. When they are willing to pay that premium for growth in all sectors of the economy, then the new trending market will begin and the consolidation will be over.

For large markets such as the United States and Japan, that state could take a long time to present itself. These are not economies that turn on a dime, as there are too many oxen to be gored, too many competing political agendas, and too much red tape to be unwound without a massive political or social upheaval.

Where Are They Now?

I've stated in this chapter that I feel we are currently in a broadly defined range-bound market between 800 and 1550 on the S&P 500. I believe we are likely to stay in this range for the next 10 years barring unprecedented monetary inflation. The effects of the E.C.B. and Federal Reserve's quantitative easing programs could be greater than just offsetting deflating asset prices. In principle, P/Es go from below average to average and then to below average. Taking a look at the last long-term sideways market, we did not see P/Es drop from their high back to the long-term mean, around 15, and then bounce higher again to resume the bull market. The U.S. market spent nearly half of that 16-year period with the average P/E ratio on the S&P 500 being below the mean. Again, it takes a long time and a number of changing factors to resume the bull market.

In recent memory, even though P/Es briefly visited below-average territory during the recession of 2008–10, I am not convinced that was enough of a dip to spur the end of the current consolidation.

To be clear, I use the term P/E when looking at the broader market. I am referring to normalized P/Es, which are a 10-year moving average of the annual P/E ratios. The reason for this is to smooth out seasonality effects and shorter-term cyclical behavior.

Profit margins are a strong determinant of near-term P/E. Right now margins are very high, unsustainably so in my opinion. Margins also have historical norms, and when there is high deviation from those norms, reversals are likely. Therefore, while stock prices with respect to forward 12-month earnings do not look that expensive, they are predicated on sustaining a higher growth rate than is practicable.

By computing P/E ratios based on 10-year trailing earnings we more accurately capture the value picture within the market. In this way, earnings now encompass the entire economic cycle, replete with two forays toward the edges of the market's broad range (800 and 1550 on the S&P 500). Historically speaking, the average P/E ratio based on 10-year trailing earnings has been about 18, which is slightly higher than the twelve-month trailing earnings. As I write this, the P/E is close to 25 times earnings.

Stocks are not cheap in mid-2012, especially when compared with wage growth.

If anything, by historical norms, P/Es are now rather expensive, which reinforces my view that we are nowhere near the end of this range-bound market. Current events being what they are, there are real structural issues that still have to be worked through before the first-tier, developed countries can start another bull market.

This means that in this environment it is even more important to pick your stocks carefully. It is also why I moved to a frontier market like Vietnam, where the prospects of growth are higher due to much better macroeconomic conditions. In Europe and the United States, there exists a debt and regulatory burden that will take years to sort through. While they have many advantages, especially in terms of infrastructure for large capital projects, those projects come with enormous regulatory costs.

After my second round of crashing out of the market, I had to go back to work, putting what I'd learned into practice and rebuilding my personal balance sheet. A lot of the ideas that are presented in this book and this chapter come out of that time in 2009 when I was working at a securities company in Ho Chi Minh City. The experience of beginning in an environment that was focused on serving the broader interests of the clientele as well as improving the company's infrastructure was not only rewarding but it was an eye-opener for me.

I learned how to become extremely picky in my analysis of which stocks were worth my investment, and I trade with the goal of accumulating them through time. All of this discussion about consolidating markets is to create a set of tools you can use to accumulate great companies at dirt-cheap prices and get paid to do so by collecting strong dividend payments. Those stocks that have been ignored by the general market during the corrective chop of a range-bound market will become the stars of the next bull market. They already had great earnings and dividends when no one was looking and the economy was a mess. Once the economy gets uncorked, the roads get cleared, and money begins flowing into the market, you will potentially be sitting on a large pile of the best stocks, which will give you the highest probability of beating the index rise by a wider margin.

Let's say that stock prices over the course of a bull market quadruple over a 15-year period. For the S&P 500, that would be a move from 1600 to 6400 if and when the next bull market occurs. By having played the range-bound market that preceded it with any degree of agility, you should expect to see gains far higher than that based on your initial outlay; 6 times? 8 times? 10 times? The number is up to you.

Trading and investing are different processes but, as we've discussed, principles of the former can be applied to the goals of the latter. Jim Rogers is famous for saying that he's a miserable trader and market timer and yet is a phenomenally successful investor. In my experience, Mr. Rogers is being too modest; understanding the current market conditions within their historical context is one of the cornerstones to being a good market timer.

I'm basing my analysis of the markets on the past 100 years or so, which coincides with the rise of central banking as a major factor in the functioning of markets and governments that regulate them. While the statistics geek in me would prefer data that stretched back to the Roman Empire, if one has to take a data set as small as this one, at least the major factors behind the data are relatively constant.

The Edge of Value

While Jim Rogers considers himself a terrible market timer he is one of the great value investors of all time. We use the term *value* a lot. But what is it, really? The whole of the economics profession has been obsessed with the definition of value for centuries, before economics was really even considered an intellectual discipline separate from anything else. If we look at auction market theory (AMT) closely, we can infer that it is a system based not on any empirical value but rather a collectively subjective one. Value, ultimately, from a trader or investor perspective, is whatever the market says it is at that moment in time.

The market attempts, through myriad transactions, to figure out what the value of a stock should be at any given point in time. Fundamental analysis is at its core a system of defining the value of a stock based on the financial numbers that the company provides us on a quarterly, semi-annual, or annual basis. Finance and M.B.A. programs spend a lot of time teaching students (young and old) different ways to value a company based on the type of business it is, where it is in its life cycle, what market it is in, and so on.

Financial instruments like bonds and derivatives (think options contracts or interest-rate swaps) are valued based on a variety of models that rest on a number of assumptions that are thought to impute the future value of the instrument based on a number of changing conditions (e.g., time). CAPM (capital asset pricing model) and Black-Scholes are examples of models for assessing the value of these types of assets. If you want to trade them, whether you agree with their premises or not, it is incumbent upon you to know how they work and why because the rest of the market is using them to figure out what value should be.

It is our job as fundamental analysts to figure out if there are reasons why the value of a stock or financial instrument will go up over time. Value investors attempt to discover that by looking at some financial statistic or ratio that correlates well with stocks outperforming the underlying index over time, generating alpha.

Joel Greenblatt, value investor and author of the *Little Book That Beats the Market* (Wiley, 2005), stated recently that the reason that most people fail at value investing is simply because they don't actually practice it. Value investing is predicated on the idea that the market has fundamentally undervalued a stock because some ratio or set of ratios about a company are below a certain value, which means to them that the market is mispricing the stock.

Therefore, if you buy the stock at that price, eventually, and more often than not, you will be rewarded with the market waking up to the arbitrage present and seeking to fill it. Greenblatt's contention is that his willingness to stick to his value criteria is his edge, saying in effect that the average person does not hold a position long enough to realize the strength of the value investing methodology.

That may very well be. I'm not here to impugn anyone's preferred approach to value investing. But investing, to me, is far more than just finding value in a numeric sense. Yes, I could agree with him that company XYZ is undervalued, but that still doesn't mean that the stock is a good buy. It may well be at some point, but it may not be because, ultimately, value is a subjective thing. Nothing has intrinsic value; not even gold. Value is what we perceive it to be and what we hold in higher esteem than the money we currently have. If that were not the case we wouldn't part with our money. I believe that fundamental value investing attempts too strongly to reduce the markets to objective values and, in doing so, creates a confirmation bias in the name of trying to be objective. So do, by the way, derivative pricing models like Black-Scholes.

The statement that the market can stay irrational far longer than you can stay solvent is a cliché for a reason.

It's true.

This is why fund managers whose priorities are to their business and clients may not be able to engage in the kind of value investing behavior Greenblatt is suggesting beats the market more consistently than anything else. And, in a way, he may be right. But, here's the rub: If everyone acted like him, he would no longer have his edge, which in the end is his point, to be fair.

But, that said, he is still taking on opportunity risk that he does not have to. If the market disagrees with you at a particular time about a stock's value, why on earth would you invest in something that has a short-term probability of going down in price in the next month just because your model says it's undervalued by 15 percent and that's your threshold? If the market is going to discount the stock to 30 percent, why would you take a position that you know has a high probability of losing 15 percent before it makes you a dime? Why would you expose yourself to the risks of something going wrong that is beyond the company's control? Toyota's fall after the Fukushima nuclear disaster comes to mind.

To me, true value investing must marry not only the numeric valuation models that reveal the strength of the company's business (of which Greenblatt's method is a good example) but also the timing of when the market's collective perception of the company's value has changed from bearish to bullish. And this is why I advocate the use of the opening range the way that I do, beyond the scope of its original intended use, which was for a particular session or day of trading. By approaching the markets both as a trader and as a fundamental analyst, one can raise the probability that every long-term investment has a maximal chance of capturing the value presented by the market's mispricing of a stock with the least amount of potential loss of time. This is my edge, restated.

I don't think I should ever put my capital at risk in a situation where I am playing longer odds than I could be. In this way, trading is not like poker, because if the market does not present an opportunity to my satisfaction, I can choose to not play.

All choices carry with them an opportunity cost of time. Choosing to do one thing (e.g., write this book) meant that I didn't do every other possible activity with my time that I could have. Again, this is a fundamental precept of economics, and it is what drives people to act: the scarcity of their time. Your investment capital, being an extension of you and fulfilling your future needs, operates under the same principle, so working toward optimizing its use should be your goal, and if that means learning how to refine your entry points into and out of markets, then so be it.

The Great One

Before I wrap this up I want to go back in time once more. There is one more story in my life that I believe has significance and will shed some light as to why and how my life has turned out the way it has and how it can help you.

When I was eight I entered a competition that gave me the opportunity to win a Wayne Gretzky rookie card. Now, if you are neither Canadian nor a card collector you may not realize just how big a deal this was. The last time one of them traded, back in 2011, it went for $94,613. To win it, all I had to do was roll a die six times and get a six every time—that's six sixes in a row.

You can find out what the odds are against rolling six consecutive sixes with a very simple calculation. The probability of it's happening on any one throw is 1 in 6 (16.666 percent). The probability of it's happening six times in a row is $1/6^6$ or 1 divided by $6 \times 6 \times 6 \times 6 \times 6 \times 6$ or 1/46,656. So there was a 0.002 percent chance that when I walked up to the counter and rolled that die for the first time that I would be walking out of that place with the card in my hand. This is no different than throwing six dice at the same time and rolling any specific combination. The probability is the same.

So when the last die came up a six and I won the card, I was just so excited to have it, I didn't take in the significance of it or just how unlikely an outcome it was. What that moment reinforced for me was a number of things both good and bad. It instilled in me that sense of the possible, the childish sense of anything still being possible. But at the same time it reinforced the idea that the big trade was not only possible; it wasn't that hard to pull off.

When we then fast-forward to my first foray into the capital markets, Wayne Gretzky, the Great One, is sitting on my shoulder, trying to remind me that what makes one a success is not the randomness of a roll of the dice but rather diligence, hard work, and, in Gretzky's case, a selflessness that allowed him to amass more than twice the number of assists as goals. In other words, it's not just about me. I wasn't charmed, just lucky. Gretzky wasn't charmed. He worked hard for everything he achieved.

So I went into that first trade looking to win the game without working for it. If you are a fan of the show *Top Gear* you know that Jeremy Clarkson has been known to ask on occasion, "How hard can it be?" just before something both horrible and very entertaining happens.

Unfortunately, in our case no one is going to make a reality show about our trading foibles. That first loss in the markets was a wake-up call about how much work lay ahead of me—and I'd like to believe that I was up to the task. What that initial round of study and execution taught me is that the big trade is out there but the last thing you can do is to plan for it.

If you've read this far, I think you will realize that many of the setups I've described have their risk and their reward clearly delineated, or at least easily calculable. The trades themselves may only net you a 4 or 8 percent gain, but that is what the market is willing to give you at that point in time. Be thankful for the opportunity to make that amount and walk away with your profit. There will always be another trading opportunity to make another 4 percent.

Baseball is not won with home runs. Professional poker players play Limit Texas Hold'em to make the mortgage payment. Professional traders hedge their risk and submit to the will of the market. Of course, we are bombarded with images and stories that entice us to believe that life is more like my brush with the Great One than it is about the day-to-day application of discipline. TV and film tell outlandish stories of these catastrophic occurrences. My winning that card could easily be the genesis for an entire movie script, whether it is the inciting incident for the rest of the story or the *deus ex machina* that gets our hero out of the jam he's in depends entirely on the movie. Advertising tells you that if you buy this thing, it'll make you a better person, capable of superhuman feats of derring-do. It is the job of that form of communication to appeal to our dreams, our sense of wonder, and our desire to better ourselves. It is the essence of all human action, after all, to turn what is into what will be. But at the same time it is important to temper that with expectations that are reasonable and within the realm of the possible.

I'm not saying don't dare to dream.

The essence of entrepreneurship is taking the risk of building something that didn't exist and finding out if there is a market for it so you can profit by creating something that other people feel they need, improving their lives through your actions. Trading and investing, however, is not the same thing for most people. It is not entrepreneurship, which begins with a dream and an idea. The quicker you can purge your dreams from your trading the more successful your trading will be.

In other words what I'm saying is the big trade isn't the outlier; it isn't being the guy smart enough to buy Apple at $9 per share when the company hit rock bottom—but if you are that guy, more power to you. The big trade is the one you make that allows you the opportunity to make the next one. Because, who knows? The probability it will be the big trade is low, but it isn't zero—and that makes all the difference in the world.

Summary

- Central banks have made traditional bear markets a thing of the past. Instead, we have grinding sideways markets that can last a generation.
  - Whether you agree or not, central banks' policy affects your trades.

- The misallocation of capital needs to be worked off, creating pockets of recovery during low-growth periods.
  - Capital is slowly being reallocated to the productive and needed sectors of the economy once the distorted industries begin failing.
  - P/Es will contract over time and investors will become even pickier about their stocks because they are poorer as well.
    - Demand higher value (i.e., higher earnings) before buying.
- The S&P is in a broadly defined sideways market between 800 and 1550.
  - It will be for a long time yet, so be patient.
- Marrying fundamental analysis, obsessed with value, with precise market timing can create extremely powerful returns with known risk profiles and low opportunity cost in waiting to get paid.
- Getting lucky once does not mean you are a great trader or that you have a magic touch.
  - Wayne Gretzky made the game of hockey look easy because he practiced harder than everyone else.
- The big trade is the one that allow you to make the next trade.

Chapter 6

Closing Arguments

The strong man is the one who is able to intercept at will the communication between the senses and the mind.
— *Napoleon Bonaparte*

Crossing the Great Stream

When I started working on this book, I did not realize how much things would change while the process was going on. While I was and am grateful for the opportunities I've had since the phone call I received coming home from my grandmother's funeral, I was beginning to feel restless again, not unlike the time before I moved here to Vietnam in the first place. This book, along with other complementary projects, was to form the basis for creating the next chapter in my life.

In working on those projects, I came to realize something about knowledge and how to use it to achieve my goals. We've talked at length about how we learn and then apply that learning to trading, as that is the focus of the book: to improve your skill set in relation to how the market operates. But the lessons, obviously, are more general than that, or at least I hope they are.

We are living in an age of massive upheaval in so many sectors of the economy because of the rise of the Internet and computing power that has changed the opportunities for communication between people. This has affected the speed at which the markets digest new data, the way the markets trade, and how we as investors and entrepreneurs act in relation to all of this new information.

And we do so solely for the purpose of conserving the one truly scarce resource we all share: our time. We've discussed a lot of concepts about the psychology of the markets and how I believe is the best course of action in trading them. But we haven't touched on the philosophy of economics itself, and what ultimately drives us to do the things we do with our lives.

In an earlier section, I made the point, in passing, that our goal when we act is to turn the present into the future we want to experience. This applies to all of your decisions from the trivial to the grandiose. We tend to only remember (or want to remember) the big decisions—quitting your very successful job and traveling halfway around the world comes to mind—but the little ones matter as well.

For some people, building connections is difficult, and sharing information in public is the furthest thing from their frame of reference. These are people who will lurk on public message boards or social media sites without ever once feeling the need or desire to make their views public. For others, the idea of doing so is as natural as drinking a glass of water.

In the end, though, it became very obvious to me that my original goal when I came to Vietnam was the wrong goal to seek. I was thinking in terms of traditional forms of mass communication (e.g., radio, TV, etc.) when I should have been thinking about the revolution happening in viral and personal communications. I had picked the wrong venue for the wrong market at the wrong time. Is it any wonder then why it failed?

My expertise did not lie in this field. It didn't lie in graphic design, lighting, sound editing, film, and TV production. Despite my best intentions, I had placed myself in a position that was going to fail. Had I consulted the I Ching, a form of divinatory practice involving 64 hexagrams, I would have likely been shown hexagram 6, Sung: .

Stepping back and looking at it now, it's plain that I knew markets, not media. And since I began working in Vietnam, it has become apparent that I learned something about communication; I had just picked the wrong format.

> CONFLICT. *You are sincere and are being obstructed. A cautious halt halfway brings good fortune, going through to the end brings misfortune. It furthers one to see the great man. It does not further one to cross the great water.*

As my restlessness grew with my situation, I knew I wanted something different and had to find a way out of where I was. I'm thankful that the communications platform of the Internet had matured to the point of allowing that to happen. When I think about the possibilities of social media, it becomes readily apparent that the audience you want to attract is out there if you are willing to put in the time to try and find them. The more you do so, the more you are yourself (for better or worse), the more opportunities will come your way.

Armed with a blog and an attitude, I began the process of building a new form of media company that could reach out to fulfill my original goal of building a financial information network in Vietnam and Southeast Asia. It started with just me, a keyboard, some free blogging software, and the chutzpah to think that my ideas were worth promulgating in order to reach out to the world in a way that I didn't see happening from anyone else. I had initial plans that were very targeted, but they quickly did not survive contact with the enemy.

And I was smart enough to go along with it. So, now, as opposed to conflict, the I Ching's hexagram 6, I was looking at following, hexagram 17:

FOLLOWING has supreme success. Perseverance furthers. No blame.

In order to succeed, I had to fail. I didn't have to invent the world from whole cloth; I just had to ride the current wave and find my place within it. I didn't have to create the technology that allowed a guy sitting in his apartment in Ho Chi Minh City to influence a person reading an article in Edmonton; I just had to figure out how best to use it. The heavy lifting had already been done, and now it was just a matter of setting down to working on it.

I knew markets and I had opinions on them, especially in Vietnam, which was so unknown to the people in the West. In the United States, where many people's only connection to Vietnam comes from a movie screen or History Channel documentary, even average information about Vietnamese markets would be looked on as enlightening.

I realized that disruptive technology or a catastrophic event wasn't the key to success but rather taking the existing technology and leveraging it to its fullest. Yes, the world was disrupted with the automobile, but not at first. It took the assembly line, itself a disruptive invention, to truly take the technology and change the world.

But even before Henry Ford began the process of revolutionizing transportation, there was the horse, which, by then,

Closing Arguments

was anything but disruptive technology. It was the Mongols who took the horse to its absolute limit. The horse was the undisputed champion of terrestrial travel for hundreds of years, and yet the Mongols leveraged their capabilities in such a way as to build an empire based on their far superior implementation of travel by horseback. It gave them unprecedented mobility and freedom from the normal logistical supply chain, which limited movement of armies, allowing them to travel as much as 100 miles per day in the 13th century.

While the assembly line was a great piece of disruptive technology, it reached its limit rather quickly in terms of production logistics. Once the discrete task model was mastered, it was subjected to the limitations of individuals' performance and training. Toyota's production system strategy of Kaizen has now been codified as Lean manufacturing and has fundamentally changed the way everyone does business. But, in the beginning, only Toyota built things that way, and it gave them a tremendous advantage in the marketplace for nearly a generation. It also had a trickle-down effect into the entire automotive supply chain, raising the quality and lowering the costs of component parts for their competitors, even if they were assembling them in a less-efficient manner. While Toyota didn't invent assembly line manufacturing, they did take it to its logical conclusion in the same way that the Mongols did with horse travel.

What does this have to do with me and my projects? Simply put, I didn't invent Twitter or hypertext, but I did see the opportunity to optimize the means by which someone could reach the maximal potential audience quickly and without much overhead to bring much-needed market information to people who would never otherwise be exposed to it. In this way, I can serve investors' interests and bring the greatest amount of value to them so they can make more and better decisions about the markets they are trading or thinking about trading. While I am writing this, I do not think the effects on the markets of Southeast Asia have been fully realized, but if I continue to *follow* where the stream takes me, I'm sure that that whatever I'm capable of producing will come to fruition.

Which brings me to my last point for this section; you may find that you are not a great trader and that my approach to trading could not help you there, but that doesn't mean my job stops at that water's edge. My hope is that my story helps you to realize that your stream is yours and that my struggles as a trader and entrepreneur can assist you in navigating it successfully.

Pressing the Issues

Having gone from being a successful prop trader to head of institutional by way of a failed media enterprise, I've come to where I am right now, synergizing all of those skills into an independent venture. As I said in the last section, I chose the web as the means to find and build an audience above and beyond my current list of professional contacts and clients, seeing where it would take me. The hope, of course, was to impress so many high-net-worth individuals that they would want to put their trust in me to manage their money for them, shifting my focus then from the sell side of the business (being a broker and pushing financial products) to the buy side of the business (asset management and financial advice). What I found out about the buy side is both surprising, if not a little disturbing, and not unlike the issues plaguing the sell side of the industry. Of course, my desire was to promote the very best ideas I had, naively thinking that quality is a thing that sells itself; if you build it, they will eventually come. While this is certainly true for the most part, it does not necessarily follow that if you have great content, it will get noticed by sheer force of its own weight. You need some form of marketing.

The internet is filled to the brim with information that, no matter how good, needs as much help as possible to cut through the haze and rise above that of others attempting the same thing, so as many people as possible can see what it is that you have to offer. Since their time is very scarce, finding people who care about what you might have to say isn't even the beginning. You still have to convince them somehow to give you the 15 minutes of their time to read an article or blog post you've written and consider it.

When you stop to think about it, it's a really daunting task, but the proof is out there that it is possible. Not only is it possible, but with the right plan of attack, it can be extremely lucrative. I hadn't really thought that it could be from the outset—as I said, my initial goal was to drive people to want to invest with me. The side benefit of being able to build a quickly profitable business was that it was paying me to allow my ideas to germinate in the minds of those I'd reached.

So out of necessity, I began building syndication partnerships with as many media companies as I could, which was fantastic but at the same time it uncovered that problem I alluded to earlier. Everyone is in essentially the same business I was: We were all attempting to drive as many eyeballs to our sites as possible, but to do that meant writing about the things that people were interested in. My initial interest was in telling the story of what I felt were the great investment opportunities in Vietnam, but there's a catch-22 in that. You can't tell Vietnam's story without devoting time to it, but at the same time very few people are interested in it. Editors from every site I've worked with have all said some variation on, "Great article, Peter, but it needs more relevant tickers." And so the trap was sprung. The noise trade had become *The Big Trade* in essence.

I don't blame the editors for this; they are trying to drive advertising revenue and solicit subscriptions from readers and the like. I completely understand this because I am in the same position on the other side of the transaction. I can tell you that the first time I wrote about Apple for AlphaVN and it got distributed through the Stocktwits network, I got caught up in the huge traffic (for me) that it drew. Even though the article was slanted toward Southeast Asia and how that was driving the possibility of Apple's growth, it was still far afield of where I had originally intended to go.

This is the problem with all of this and why as a trader or investor you need to be aware of it. The entire media complex is an echo chamber that creates a self-selection bias toward certain companies or regions of the world at the expense of the rest of them. It highlights one of the real problems with fundamental analysis on the sell side in that the attention is on all of the big-cap stocks of potentially marginal fundamental value (though not necessarily true of Apple in this instance). This happens both because that's where brokers find it easy to sell to customers and where the research departments can find the most readily available information. This is especially true in emerging and frontier markets like Vietnam. All the attention is on the Vincoms or the Hoang Anh Gia Lais and not on the Minh Phu Seafoods. Even if you can get people to invest in Vietnam, they feel a certain level of comfort knowing they are buying a large-cap stock that a lot of other people own as opposed to going off the board, so to speak, and putting a few dollars down on a company with great fundamentals, trading at a multiple of four and paying an 8 to 10 percent dividend. I can't tell you I heard some variation on the following: *Nope, Peter, really, I'll take a thousand shares of the bloated bureaucracy trading at a multiple of 30, paying 3 percent.*

So the media that we are selling our research to is incentivizing us to discuss lesser-quality opportunities, reinforcing the status quo and ensuring that investment capital does not leak away from these high-profile companies who may or may not be advertisers with them in the first place. It builds in a selection bias, which generates the very noise it's trying to capitalize on.

It's not all bad, mind you, but it has an effect on perception. No one is immune from this. In the end, what I am advising is for investors to be aware of this bias and keep a weather eye on what they read. Remember to consider the source, do your own due diligence, and always remain a little skeptical about why a particular piece of research exists.

The Point of the Journey Is Not to Arrive

My journey has been an interesting one. From over-enthusiastic novice to restless veteran, mine is a blue-jeans-to-BMW-and-back-again story that is not nearly over yet. Thank goodness. If I had walked away at first, taking my lumps and telling myself that I was not good enough, then today I wouldn't be where I am. If I had not met Anhtoan and gotten his help in ways that I don't think I'll ever adequately be able to repay, you wouldn't be reading this. And I certainly wouldn't be happy.

For all of my time and diligence, study and hard work, I've done it with the goal of leading my life my way. The markets have only been there to facilitate that goal. If this book can impart one lesson to you it is that there is only one life worth living—your own. Do so in whatever manner you decide is right for you. If imparting my observations about investing and trading can help you achieve that, then we are both improved.

It is so easy to get lost in the minutia of our knowledge, become so focused on the present and the daily challenges, that it is easy to lose sight of the long-term goal. Economics and markets are not dry and dusty collections of mathematics, charts, and statistical regression models. Rather, as I touched upon earlier, they are made of the very things that define us as human beings. Those charts represent our hopes and desires, our need to turn what we have into what we want—to turn what is into what will be.

The common thread of this book is humility. In order to be a successful market operator at any level you must first admit to yourself that no matter how much you think you know, you don't know it all. Austrian economist Friedrich Hayek called this "The Information Problem." It is not possible to know everything there is to know about a particular subject any more than it is possible to know everything about the market. Without fully accepting this, and I have met so many people who have not (at times I have failed to acknowledge this idiom myself), your trading and investing will suffer.

Into this vessel of cultivated humility we have poured the core concepts of my trading method. By stressing simplicity of design and merging it with meaning-rich statistics we have created a foundation from which to base our trading decisions. This is a holistic approach to viewing markets, filtering out our subjective interpretations of what we think is happening and focusing on what we are experiencing.

The great science-fiction writer Philip K. Dick once said that "reality is that which, when you stop believing in it, doesn't go away." In the markets, as we discussed in Chapter 1, our interpretations of what reality is can lead us down blind alleys and mazes of confusion, trapping us in our desire to control that which is beyond us.

By combining auction market theory's (AMT's) focus on the supply of buyers versus sellers in the moment with opening ranges as slices of price movement, we define a state of the market that is as divorced from our interpretations as possible. Trading occurs when enough people believe the current price does not reflect reality and their collective action moves the price away from its current one.

The beauty of a system like this is that it respects everyone's different interpretation of the market without placing a value judgment on its being either right or wrong.

The market *is*. It isn't right or wrong.

Investors and traders judge the value of a stock along all different time horizons, from the ultra-short to the generationally long. The hardest part for you will be determining where your skills best fit along that spectrum of time.

If you are a long-term investor, looking at the state of the macro market will tell you how much time you have to accumulate capital while you look for your low-risk entry price. The use of opening ranges here is very powerful in determining when you should deploy your capital. AMT can tell you where the market currently is in relation to fair value. Analysis of fundamentals will, of course, influence that assessment as well. Buying good stocks with strong dividends near the low of the consolidation range is a great way to get paid to wait.

Virtual trading is an absolute prerequisite in my mind. Nothing substitutes for screen time, internalizing the rhythms of the market on an intraday and day-to-day basis. While having skin in the game does heighten your perception of what is happening, it will also confuse you until you've internalized trading setups. Your hormonal response to both winning and losing a trade is something that clouds your brain's ability to process patterns and intuit the upcoming direction and timing of a move.

Getting acquainted with how a stock is traded will save you money and heartache. Virtual trading gives you experience without the risk of losing everything while you refine your shorter-term trading strategy to accumulate your target stock. Think of this as part of your due diligence on a company, going beyond sector and financial analysis.

Rest assured, I will not be standing over your shoulder telling you that you did not execute well. There is no one you have to serve while trading other than yourself. I cannot stress this enough. I don't see myself in competition with my family, friends, or colleagues when I trade. I simply try to focus on selling without regrets, without second-guessing myself. It's my hope that, over time, you will find the best way to achieve that which is uniquely yours—your personal edge.

There is something to be said for a positive approach to trading. Child psychologists tell adults that whatever behaviors they do, they get more of from children. Parents should stress the behavior they want their child to exhibit and not dwell on that which they don't. Even as adults, we see that focusing on the negative, harping on the mistakes will sow the seeds for the next failure. However, approaching everything you do with an open mind and focusing on the positive means that success will come more often. In trading, this means you accept the profit on a good trade or exit a bad one quickly. You do not lament money "left on the table" or be angry that your perfect trading setup failed to deliver. At best I've found that only two out of three trades are successful. If you can maximize your gains on the good ones and minimize the losses on the bad ones, on balance you will come out ahead.

While the material presented here is a reflection of my ups and downs, this book is not about me. It's about you and what my experiences can do to improve your performance. As I said at the beginning of the book, I present to you who I am, for better or worse, and my hope is to draw out of you who you are.

For me, the journey to this point has been the adventure and I know myself well enough to know that I will not be able to predict what will come next. Today, it is building an investment advisory firm through social media. Tomorrow? Well, I'll leave that for tomorrow.

Summary

- All of the decisions we make have far-reaching consequences.
  - The most successful people in this field are those that leverage existing technology to its fullest instead of trying to create something new.
    - Disruptive optimization of existing technology can be beneficial.
- The financial press plays a huge role in creating perception and bias in the markets.
  - Building a company to sell content to them has made this very clear.
  - Be your own research department and question everything you read.

- Don't worry, be happy. If trading is not your thing, find that out quickly and concentrate on what you do well.
  - My life has been dominated by trading, but it may not be right for you.
  - This book can also function as a guide to assess the person managing your money.
  - Trading and investing are a means to an end, not the end itself.

Appendix A

Terms and Definitions

Alpha The measure of the performance of a stock in relation to an index over the past year. The index is defined as having an alpha of 0.

Beta The measure of the relative volatility of a stock versus an index over the past year. A beta score greater than 1 is more volatile than the index and vice versa.

Breakout The moment when a stock violates the top or bottom of an opening range or consolidation range.

Consolidation A period where the price of a stock oscillates in a range around a median value that is considered fair value.

Fair Value The mean or median of a consolidation range.

Fundamental Analysis An approach to valuation of a stock based on the financial fundamentals of the company.

GDP Gross domestic product is the sum of all goods and services produced by any country in a year.

Inside Day A trading day in which neither the high nor the low of the previous trading day was violated.

Intraday Trading Otherwise known as day-trading, is the practice of completing a trade within one trading session. There are FINRA regulations associated with this style of trading in the United States.

Market Condition From auction market theory (AMT). It is the state of the market: consolidating, trending, or transitioning from one to the other.

Multistability An aspect of perception where an ambiguous image vacillates between two equally valid interpretations.

Opening Range The price range delineated by the opening slice of a period of time from which action can be taken.

The first price hurdle a stock must overcome before reaching a target price. A slice of the price range within a bar of time.

Outside Day A trading day in which either the high or the low of the previous trading day was violated.

Quantitative Analysis Analysis of price tendencies based on past performance creating probabilities of change.

P/E Ratio (Price-to-Earnings Ratio) Earnings are reported in currency per share, the same unit as the stock. A company with $1 of earnings trading at $10 per share has a P/E of 10.

PEG Rate (Price-to-Earnings Growth Rate) The P/E divided by the projected earnings growth rate of a stock based on company guidance and analyst recommendations.

Reification An aspect of perception where the brain interprets more spatial information than is actually there.

Stop An order that is triggered to exit a trade.

Swing Trading A style of trading that seeks to profit from trends that develop over the course of multiple sessions or days.

Technical Analysis An approach to price-chart analysis that focuses on interpretation of the chart's formations. It is a catchall phrase that encompasses a wide variety of techniques.

Volume The number of shares of a stock traded during one bar on a chart.

Volume Delta The difference between the amount of volume transacted on the bid price versus the ask price. A positive delta implies more offers being lifted, meaning there are more sellers in the market. A negative delta implies more bid being hit, meaning there are more buyers in the market.

Appendix B

Trading Examples

Example 1: Consolidation Breakout from Range

In Figure B.1 and Table B.1, we come back to Apple (AAPL). At the end of the text for this example are some supporting statistics (Figure B.3), which I will refer to. After a steep sell-off during the financial crisis of 2008, AAPL spent a few months consolidating between $80 and $103 per share. Classic opening range trading would have set the month of January 2009 as the opening range, and that would have worked out just fine in the long run. The January high was $97.17, and a buy would have been made during the week of February 2, 2009, when that price was broken and Apple closed at $99.72. The weekly average range was $11.06, but the stock was not done consolidating; it spent the next two months with that trade in a losing position.

Taking the opening range concept to the next level of using the entire consolidation period as the opening range (the

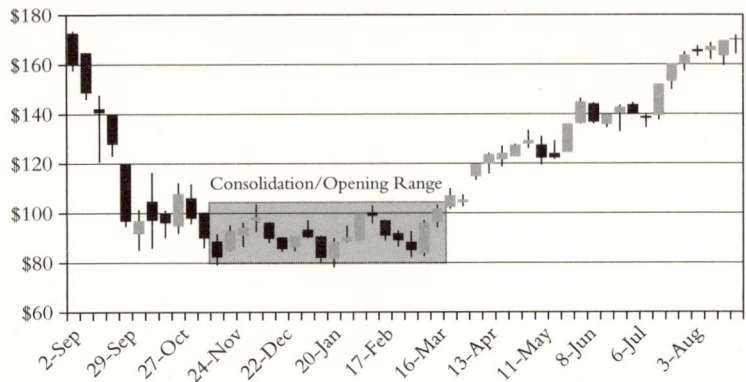

Figure B.1 AAPL 2008–2009 Weekly Chart

Table B.1 Apple 2008–09 Weekly Data

Date	Open	High	Low	Close
1/5/2009	93.17	97.17	90.04	90.58
1/12/2009	90.46	90.99	80.05	82.33
1/20/2009	81.93	90	78.2	88.36
1/26/2009	88.86	95	88.3	90.13
2/2/2009	89.1	100	88.9	99.72
2/9/2009	100	103	95.77	99.16
2/17/2009	96.87	97.04	89	91.2
2/23/2009	91.65	92.92	86.51	89.31
3/2/2009	88.12	92.77	82.33	85.3
3/9/2009	84.18	97.2	82.57	95.93
3/16/2009	96.53	103.48	94.18	101.59
3/23/2009	102.71	109.98	101.75	106.85

SOURCE: Data from Yahoo! Finance.

box on Figure B.1) we can see that AAPL closed during the week of March 16 at $101.59, but it had made a new high for the year during that week, which put the stock in a high probability position to break higher the following week. Using the high from March 16 as our opening range, AAPL opened on March 23 at $102.71. The opening range can be the difference,

$0.77, and we can ask the question: *If AAPL moves up $0.77 what's the probability it moves up $3.00 before the end of the week?*

The answer is 70.1 percent (see Figure B.3). So, we know that if AAPL breaks above $103.50 that there is a 70.1 percent chance it will go to $105.71 and a 5.3 percent chance that it will break the previous week's low of $94.18. Once it closes the week above $103.50 and the consolidation area high goes back to November 2008, taking a position there presents a high probability setup for an extended run higher. This is the third bar up after a three-week downtrend within the consolidation zone and at this point we can be content to hold the stock until we see a two-bar reversal to the downside.

That occurs just barely the week of May 18, when AAPL closes down $0.23 for the week at $122.50. If one cashes out there completely, it would have been for a $19.00 gain or 18.4 percent. One could have sold half the position into such a weak second reversal bar since it is an inside week, but in that month AAPL is down over the open by more than $6 and it's average move below the open is $11.39 in any given month. There is a 65 percent chance that the stock could move down another $4.00.

One the one hand, the weekly stats are telling you that, of the 11 times AAPL has had two down weeks in a row, 8 of them continued the trend. So, at that point there is still plenty of downside possible in the short term. On the other hand, moving out and looking at the monthly chart tells you that there is nothing to worry about in the broader sense. There was a monthly break of the previous high, AAPL opened the month above the previous month's close, and the probabilities were high that the $4–5 that the stock could drop would be all that would happen before the uptrend would continue. If you shift your focus on this trade to a monthly perspective AAPL does not give you a compelling reason to sell until May 2010 (Figure B.2), after a gain of more than $150, nearly 150 percent as opposed to 18–20 percent.

APPENDIX B

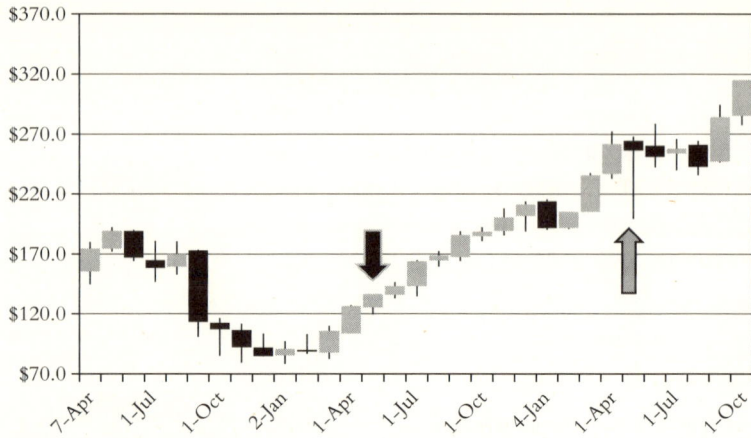

Figure B.2 AAPL Monthly Chart 2008–2010

AAPL Weekly Statistics						
	% Probability	# of Points		What If?	# of times	
Range		11.06	Up Move			
Avg. High Move		5.10	Opening Range	0.77	107	
Break Prev High	51.5%		Target Move	3	75	
Avg. Low Move		-5.96	% Probability	70.09%		
Break Prev. Low	37.1%			What If?	# of times	
Total Breaks	88.6%		Down Move			
Inside Day	12.9%		Opening Range	-6	46	
High + Low Break	5.3%		Target Move	-10	28	
Open is High	0.0%		% Probability	60.87%		
Open is Low	0.8%					

Uptrend Length	# of Times	Reversal %	Downtrend Length	# of Times	Reversal %
1	28		-1	27	
2	18	35.7%	-2	11	59.3%
3	13	27.8%	-3	8	27.3%
4	6	53.8%	-4	4	50.0%
5	3	50.0%	-5	1	75.0%
6	2	33.3%	-6	1	0.0%

AAPL Monthly Statistics					
	% Probability	# of Points		What If?	# of Times
Range		21.75	Up Move Opening Range	1	39
Avg. High Move		10.36	Target Move	5	28
Break Prev High	61.9%		% Probability	71.79%	
Avg. Low Move		-11.39			
Break Prev. Low	38.1%				
Total Breaks	7.1%				# of
Inside Day	7.1%		Down Move Opening	What If?	Times
High + Low Break	7.1%	Avg Move	Range	-6	20
Open is High	0.0%		Target Move	-10	13
Open is Low	0.0%		% Probability	65.00%	
Uptrend Length	# of Times	Reversal %	Downtrend Length	# of Times	Reversal %
1	10		-1	9	
2	4	60.0%	-2	5	44.4%
3	4	0.0%	-3	1	80.0%
4	2	50.0%	-4	1	0.0%
5	2	0.0%	-5	0	100.0%

Figure B.3 Supporting Statistics for AAPL

Example 2: Consolidation Breakdown—Going Short

The next example is the exact opposite of the first one. I've added the relevant statistics for the discussion at the end of the section (Figure B.6), and all statistics mentioned here are drawn from there. Here we have Ford (NYSE: F), which rallied until the middle of January 2012 and then hit a wall of sellers at $13 but also saw buyers coming in near $12 for nearly three months. The monthly statistics say the average range for F is $2.03, so this is clearly abnormal behavior, trading within $1.10 for three months. Moreover, the weekly statistics say that the average range is $0.95 and the stock hasn't moved more than

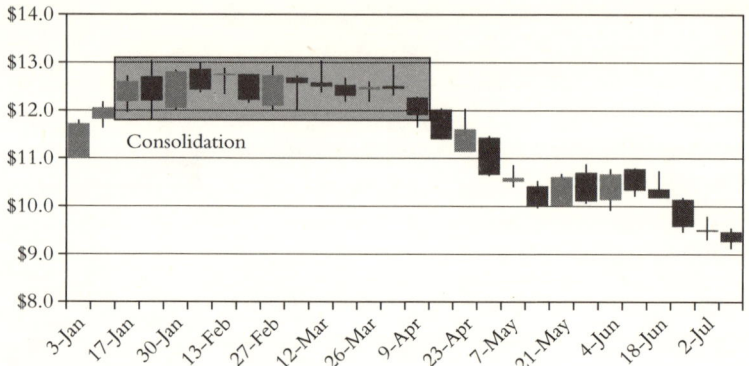

Figure B.4 F 2012 Consolidation Breakdown Example

half of that per week over the past five weeks at the point in early April when the selling starts.

Table B.2 has the data for the period of time we'll be examining. The week of April 9 opens below the low of the previous week, which yields a high-probability setup of a $0.50 move on average below the open. F opened at $12.26, which puts your first target at $12.00. If the price reaches $12.00, however, there is a 56.4 percent chance that the stock will drop another $0.24, which would violate the low of the consolidation range. It sells down to and through that level on April 10 on twice the normal volume. Here your $0.26 opening range is being used as an early warning system of a potential breakdown from a range-bound market. Moreover, the average weekly range is telling you that there's a high probability that the stock will not move much above its opening price.

Going short on the weekly close below $12.00 at $11.92 would be a high-percentage move. Ford opens the next week at $12.01. There is a 66.1 percent chance that if it moves $0.10 above the open that it can eclipse the previous week's high, which would be a sign of buyers coming in to support the range. That does not happen; it reaches just $12.05 and then sells off. It closes at $11.88 on Monday April 16. On the 17th it opens at $11.98 and reaches a high of $12.00, having a 77.7

Table B.2 Supporting Data for F

Date	Open	High	Low	Close
3/26/2012	12.45	12.61	12.18	12.48
4/2/2012	12.5	12.95	12.32	12.47
4/9/2012	12.26	12.29	11.65	11.92
4/16/2012	12.01	12.05	11.39	11.41
4/23/2012	11.15	12.04	11.15	11.6
4/30/2012	11.42	11.47	10.63	10.67
5/7/2012	10.53	10.86	10.4	10.58
5/14/2012	10.41	10.53	9.96	10.01
5/21/2012	10.02	10.68	10	10.6
5/29/2012	10.69	10.88	10.06	10.12
6/4/2012	10.15	10.78	9.91	10.66

SOURCE: Data from Yahoo! Finance.

percent chance of besting Monday's high of $12.05. It fails to do so and sells off below $11.90. Now your odds are improving that this will be another down week and you can let the trade ride until a two-week reversal pattern emerges.

The following week there is a rally, but it cannot eclipse the previous week's high. As of this writing there has not been a suitable exit point from this trade. If anything, there is another opportunity in June to put on another short (marked with a black arrow in Figure B.5) without having covered the original. The setup for that short is nearly identical to the first one.

This brings up the point that some exit points are more difficult to determine than others. There was a five-week consolidation in May through June (marked with an arrow in Figure B.5) that is evident on a daily or weekly chart (data not shown) that brings up the possibility of your money sitting dead and waiting for something to happen, which may very well be a higher turn. Your daily data may give you the clues you need about the disposition of the market, but those signals carry less weight than looking at larger, not smaller, blocks of time. Taking a look at F from a monthly perspective, Figure B.5, tells you clearly that the bearish trend was not at all broken by

APPENDIX B

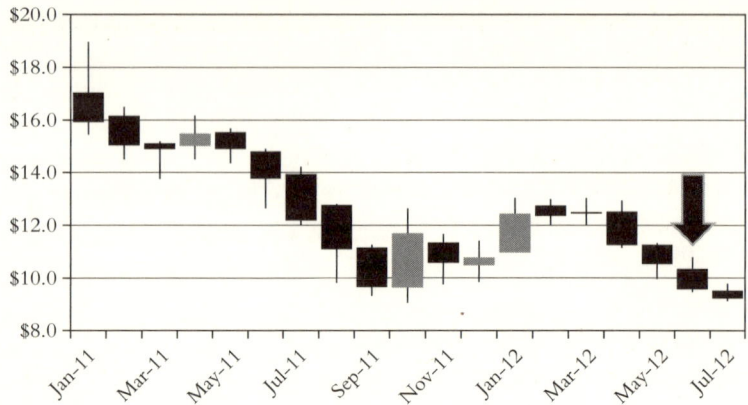

Figure B.5 F Monthly Chart 2011–2012

Ford Daily Statistics						
	% Probability	# of Points				
Range		0.39	Up Move	What If?	# of times	
Avg. High Move		0.16	Opening Range	0.02	220	
Break Prev High	43.3%		Target Move	0.08	171	
Avg. Low Move		-0.23	% Probability	77.73%		
Break Prev. Low	32.0%					
Total Breaks	92.1%		Down Move	What If?	# of times	
Inside Day	13.1%		Opening Range	-0.05	223	
High + Low Break	5.2%	0.41	Target Move	-0.2	110	
Open is High	4.0%	-0.4	% Probability	49.33%		
Open is Low	0.4%	-0.4				
Uptrend Length	# of Times	Reversal %	Downtrend Length	# of Times	Reversal %	
1	60		1	60		
2	25	58.3%	-2	35	41.7%	
3	2	92.0%	-3	20	42.9%	
4	2	0.0%	-4	11	45.0%	
5	1	50.0%	-5	7	36.4%	
6	1	0.0%	-6	4	42.9%	

Ford Weekly Statistics						
	% Probability	# of Points				
						# of times
Range		0.95	Up Move	What If?		120
Avg. High Move		0.45	Opening Range	0.04		
Break Prev High	49.2%		Target Move	0.31		69
Avg. Low Move		-0.50	% Probability	57.50%		
Break Prev. Low	45.5%					
						# of times
Total Breaks	94.7%		Down Move	What If?		
Inside Day	11.4%		Opening Range	-0.18		91
High + Low Break	9.8%		Target Move	-0.5		44
Open is High	1.5%		% Probability	48.35%		
Open is Low	0.0%					

Uptrend Length	# of Times	Reversal %	Downtrend Length	# of Times	Reversal %
1	29		-1	29	
2	15	48.3%	-2	14	51.7%
3	9	40.0%	-3	6	57.1%
4	5	44.4%	-4	4	33.3%
5	4	20.0%	-5	3	25.0%
6	3	25.0%	-6	2	33.3%

Figure B.6   F Daily and Weekly Statistics

that consolidation, thus confirming that the breakdown of that consolidation on the weekly chart would be another opportunity to add to your existing short if you wanted.

Example 3: Building a Trade

As opposed to going over another example of a particular trading setup, I thought it would be useful to go over the mechanics of how to build the tools you need to analyze a trade. In essence, I'm going to go over how I built the previous two examples manually without having access to an expensive data package. Keep in mind as well that there are Application Programming Interfaces (APIs) available to hook into Excel and automate the process, but I'll leave that to you to figure out.

The first step in the process is choosing a stock and looking for a particular setup you might want to trade. Examples 1 and 2 were specific types of setups that required some tracking down. In reality, you will spend some time searching for stocks with good fundamentals (or exceptionally bad ones, if you are a contrarian) that you want to take a position in. Sites like Yahoo Finance, for example, can get you data for most stocks and indexes that you may be interested in analyzing and/or trading.

This is how I built most of the examples in the book. The basic procedure is as follows:

1. Go to the stock's page.
2. Click on "Historical Prices" in the left-hand margin.
3. Enter the date range of interest along with the time period.
4. Open the data in Excel directly (there's a link at the bottom of the page—"Download to Spreadsheet"—to do that).
5. Construct the statistics for each time frame.

They will give you the data on a daily, weekly, and monthly basis for the open, high, low, close, and volume. This is pretty much all of the data you need to build your spreadsheet. The rest is building the back-tests that will yield the data you are interested in obtaining.

For this example, I'm going to use Coca-Cola (NYSE: KO). Figure B.7 is an 11-year monthly chart. A stock like KO is great for this because the data set is enormous thanks to the company's long history. Looking at its long-term chart, which was built, like most of the charts in this book, from a data set downloaded from the Internet into Excel 2010, we see that the

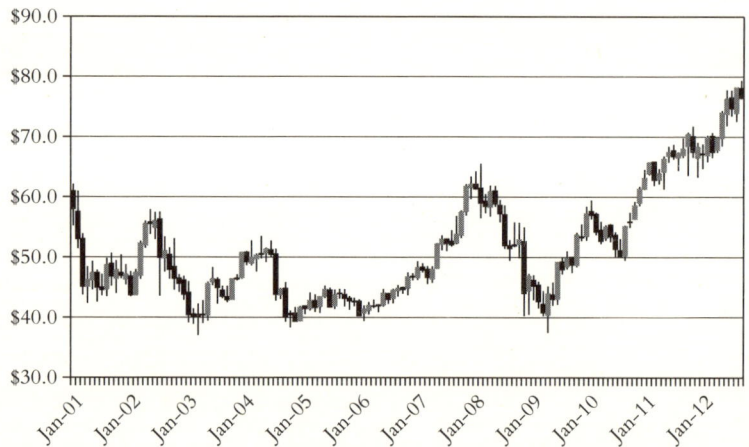

Figure B.7   KO 11-Year Monthly Chart

price has moved between $40 and $90 per share over the last 11 years, which means that the entire data set is relevant statistically. A stock that has moved a lot like AAPL is difficult to use huge data sets on because a $10 move versus a price of $80 is more significant than versus a price of $600.

To build a stock chart in Excel is very easy, but you need to have open, high, low, and closing prices. Simply reorder the data from the set from oldest to newest, then click and drag to highlight the four columns of data (open, high, low, close) and choose the chart type from the list on the ribbon. Everything after that is simple formatting.

To build a spreadsheet to analyze a stock, take the downloaded data set and copy and paste it directly into your template spreadsheet, which should have all of your statistics calculated in other columns. (See Figure B.8.)

The imported data is in the highlighted cells. The other columns will automatically update and the spreadsheet will recalculate itself, instantly yielding the data. Let's take these calculated columns in order.

- **Up or Down Day?:** An IF function subtracting the close from the open and returning 1 if true (an up day) and −1 if not true (a down day). If the close is greater than the open, then the price went up and vice versa. Returning 1 or −1 will help calculate trend length.
- **Consecutive Up Days?:** An IF function that asks if column G equals 1, then add that to the next value in column H, otherwise return 0. For cell H3, if cell G3=1, then add H4+G3, which equals 2 in this case, otherwise return 0. This will calculate the length of any uptrend in the column.
- **Consecutive Down Days?:** The same IF function as above, except that it checks for a value of −1 instead of 1. The math is exactly the same. For example, for cell I5, if cell G5 = −1, then add G5+I6, in this case −2. This calculated the length of any downtrend.

A	B	C	D	E	F	G	H	I	J	K	L	M	N
						Up or Down Day?	Consecutive Up days?	Consecutive Down days?	High Break?	Low Break?	Total Breaks	Inside Day?	High + Low Break?
Date	Open	High	Low	Close									
Jan-01	60.94	62.19	55.19	58		1	2	0	1		1		
Feb-01	57.5	60.99	51.41	53.03		1	1	0	1		1		
Mar-01	53.03	53.9	43.76	45.16		−1	0	−2	1	1	1		
Apr-01	45.16	48.45	42.37	46.19		−1	0	−1			1		
May-01	46.19	49.35	44.6	47.4		1	2	0	1		1		
Jun-01	47.4	47.9	42.59	45		1	1	0	1	1	2		1
Jul-01	45	47.2	43.65	44.6		−1	0	−1			0	1	
Aug-01	44.7	49.85	43.5	48.67		1	1	0	1	1	1		
Sep-01	48.92	50.7	45.25	46.85		−1	0	−1			1		
Oct-01	46.5	49.49	44.01	47.88		1	1	0	1	1	1		
Nov-01	47.4	50.45	46.46	46.96		−1	0	−1	1		1		
Dec-01	46.35	48.8	45.45	47.15		1	1	0	1		1		

Figure B.8 Building the Data Analysis Spreadsheet

- **High Break?:** This is an IF function that checks if the current high was higher than the previous high price. If so, return 1 and if not return nothing.
- **Low Break?:** Same as the *High Break?* calculation except it's comparing the low prices, the current versus the previous.
- **Total Breaks?:** Sums the previous two columns to find the number of breaks in that day.
- **Inside Day?:** Checks to see if *Total Breaks?* equals 0 by using an IF function. If column L = 0, then return 1, otherwise return nothing.
- **High + Low Break?:** Another IF function looking at the *total breaks* column, L, to see if both the previous high and the previous low were broken that day. If *Total Breaks?* = 2, then return 1, otherwise return nothing.

Figure B.9 is an extension of the Figure B.8, where the rest of the statistics are being calculated. Note that columns G through N are still part of the spreadsheet; they are simply hidden using Excel's hide function.

- **Range:** This is the absolute value of the difference between the closing prices between the current and previous time period.
- **High − Low:** This is the difference between that row's high and low price and it represents the breadth of prices traded during that time period.
- **Open-to-High Move:** This is the difference between the high and the open price for that row.
- **Open = High:** An IF function that compares the open and the high. If they are equal return 1, otherwise return 0 or nothing.
- **Open-to-Low Move:** This is the difference between the open and the low price for that row.
- **Open = Low?:** An IF function that compares the open and the low. If they are equal return 1, otherwise return 0 or nothing.

	A	B	C	D	E	F	O	P	Q	R	S	T	U	V	W	X	Y
1																	
2	Date	Open	High	Low	Close	Range		High-Low			Open-to-High Move		Open = High?		Open-to-Low Move	Open = Low	
3	Jan-01	60.94	62.19	55.19	58	4.97		7			1.25		0			−5.75	0
4	Feb-01	57.5	60.99	51.41	53.03	7.87		9.58			3.49		0			−6.09	0
5	Mar-01	53.03	53.9	43.76	45.16	1.03		10.14			0.87		0			−9.27	0
6	Apr-01	45.16	48.45	42.37	46.19	1.21		6.08			3.29		0			−2.79	0
7	May-01	46.19	49.35	44.6	47.4	2.4		4.75			3.16		0			−1.59	0
8	Jun-01	47.4	47.9	42.59	45	0.4		5.31			0.5		0			−4.81	0
9	Jul-01	45	47.2	43.65	44.6	4.07		3.55			2.2		0			−1.35	0
10	Aug-01	44.7	49.85	43.5	48.67	1.82		6.35			5.15		0			−1.2	0
11	Sep-01	48.92	50.7	45.25	46.85	1.03		5.45			1.78		0			−3.67	0
12	Oct-01	46.5	49.49	44.01	47.88	0.92		5.48			2.99		0			−2.49	0
13	Nov-01	47.4	50.45	46.46	46.96	0.19		3.99			3.05		0			−0.94	0
14	Dec-01	46.35	48.8	45.45	47.15	3.4		3.35			2.45		0			−0.9	0

Figure B.9 More Spreadsheet Calculations of Vital Statistics

The only things left to build are the summary statistics themselves (Figure B.10). I've presented this screenshot previously, but here it is again, and we'll go over it step by step.
Range: This is the average range of the data set, using the AVERAGE function from Excel.

- **Avg. High/Low Move:** Again, an average of the column that calculated the difference between the high/low and the open price. This tells you, on average, how far the stock will move above/below the open price in any given time period (day, week, month).
- **Break Prev High/Low?:** A sum of the column, which calculates if the previous high/low was broken that month. A SUM of the *High Break?* or *Low Break?* column. This is divided by the number of data points to yield a percentage probability.
- **Total Breaks:** A sum of the total number of times the high and low were broken divided by the number of data points in the study.
- **Inside Day:** The sum of the *Inside Day* column divided by the number of days in the study, yielding a percentage probability of an inside day occurring.
- **High + Low Break:** The sum of the *High + Low Break* column divided by the number of days in the study.
- **Open is High/Low:** The percentage probability that the open price was the high or the low for the time period in question. It is calculated by dividing the *High/Low=Open* column by the number of days in the study.

In Chapter 3 we went over the use of the COUNTIF function to sum up a conditional number of events (e.g., how many times the price rose $0.25 over the open price). All of the other statistics are built using the COUNTIF function on either the *Open-to-High Move* column or *Open-to-Low Move* column.

The uptrend and downtrend charts (Figure B.10) also use COUNTIF in the same manner, except they are looking at the

	A	B	C	D	E	F
1		% Probability	# of Points			
2						
3	Range		4.86	Up Move	What If?	# of Times
4	Avg. High Move		2.35	Opening Range	1	30
5	Break Prev High	47.6%		Target Move	5	3
6	Avg. Low Move		−2.50	% Probability	10.00%	
7	Break Prev. Low	45.2%				
8	Total Breaks	92.9%				
9	Inside Day	7.1%		Down Move	What If?	# of Times
10	High + Low Break	7.1%		Opening Range	−4	6
11	Open is High	0.0%		Target Move	−5	4
12	Open is Low	2.4%		% Probability	66.67%	
13						
14	Uptrend	# of Times	Reversal %	Downtrend	# of Times	Reversal %
15	Length			Length		
16	1	11		−1	10	
17	2	5	54.5%	−2	5	50.0%
18	3	2	60.0%	−3	3	40.0%
19	4	1	50.0%	−4	2	33.3%
20	5	1	0.0%	−5	1	50.0%
21	6	1	0.0%	−6	0	100.0%
22	7	0		−7	0	

Figure B.10 Example Layout of the Summary Stock Statistics

Consecutive Up/Down column and checking against the length specified at the beginning of the row.

From there, it is a matter of making worksheets in Excel for each time frame under study (e.g., day, week, month) and importing the data from Yahoo! Finance into them. Armed with the statistics, it is now possible to begin monitoring a stock and see where potential trading opportunities present themselves.

Appendix C

Spreadsheet Examples

For the reversal test described in Chapter 4, here are the steps to compile and create the test for a particular stock:

1. Import open, high, low, and close data for the stock from the Internet (e.g., Yahoo! Finance or Forexpros.com).
2. In the next column, set up a conditional to assess the length of an uptrend. This will return integers that will tell you the number of days the stock has gone up in a row, or 0, indicating that it went down.
   a. The calculation is: If({close} > {prev. close} then add 1 to the previous cell, otherwise return 0).
   b. If your close data is in column E and your test is in column H, the syntax would be in Excel: **IF**(E2 > E1, H1+1,0).
   c. Copy that formula down the column.

3. In the next column, set up the following conditional to select which of these days are the third in an uptrend and test the success or failure of the setup.
   a. The calculation is: If ({previous day} <> 2 return 0, if =2 then check if {today's high} > {previous high}, if it is not, return a 0, then check {the minimum of today's low plus the next two day's lows} > {the minimum of the previous 2 days' lows}, if so then return "2" otherwise "1".
      i. This first tests whether the previous two days were up days. If not, stop and return 0.
      ii. Then check today's high versus the previous high, the criteria for going long. If that is not true, return 0.
      iii. If the low and the next two lows are not lower than the low of the two reversal upticks (i.e., the two previous lows) then the setup was a success, in which case it returns 2, otherwise it failed and returns 1.
   b. Excel syntax is: **IF**({Prev. Day counter}) <>2, 0, **IF**({High}<{Previous High},0, **IF**{Min (Range of today + next 2 lows)}>{**MIN**(Range of 2 previous lows)},2,1).
      i. This will return a 0, if there was no opportunity to go long, 2 if the setup succeeded, and 1 if the stop was triggered by violating the low of the trend.
   c. Copy that formula down in the column.
4. Use a COUNTIF function covering the entire range of results obtained above to total up the number of 2 results and the number of 1 results. Use one function per cell.
   a. Excel syntax is: **COUNTIF**({cell #1: cell:#last}, 2).
5. In a third cell sum up the total number of 2's and 1's, as this tells you the number of times a trading opportunity occurred.
6. Then divide the total number of 2's by the sum to get the success rate.

Appendix D

Supporting Data for Nvidia Example in Chapter 4

APPENDIX D

	NVDA	Daily	Statistics		
	% Probability	# of Points			
Range		0.76	Up Move	What If?	# of times
Avg. High Move		0.35	Opening Range	0	246
Break Prev High	46.0%		Target Move	0.1	185
Avg. Low Move		-0.40	% Probability	75.20%	
Break Prev. Low	33.6%				
Total Breaks	97.2%		Down Move	What If?	# of times
Inside Day	11.1%		Opening Range	-0.1	205
High + Low Break	8.3%	0.80	Target Move	-0.5	66
Open is High	2.4%	-0.7	% Probability	32.20%	
Open is Low	2.8%	-0.8			

Uptrend Length	# of Times	Reversal %	Downtrend Length	# of Times	Reversal %
1	60		1	60	
2	27	55.0%	-2	34	43.3%
3	2	92.6%	-3	19	44.1%
4	1	50.0%	-4	11	42.1%
5	0	100.0%	-5	6	45.5%
6	0		-6	1	83.3%
7	0		-7	1	

Appendix D

NVDA Weekly Statistics

	% Probability	# of Points		What If?	# of times
Range		1.54	Up Move		
Avg. High Move		0.75	Opening Range	0.1	109
Break Prev High	47.7%		Target Move	0.2	95
Avg. Low Move		-0.80	% Probability	87.16%	
Break Prev. Low	47.7%			What If?	# of times
Total Breaks	95.5%		Down Move		
Inside Day	11.4%		Opening Range	-0.2	105
High + Low Break	10.6%	Avg Move	Target Move	-0.5	69
Open is High	0.0%	2.0	% Probability	65.71%	
Open is Low	3.0%	#DIV/0!			

Uptrend Length	# of Times	Reversal %	Downtrend Length	# of Times	Reversal %
1	34		-1	35	
2	14	58.8%	-2	18	48.6%
3	5	64.3%	-3	8	55.6%
4	4	20.0%	-4	5	37.5%
5	2	50.0%	-5	1	80.0%
6	1	50.0%	-6	0	100.0%

About the Author

Peter Pham is recognized worldwide as an expert consultant in global equities with 12+ years of experience in all aspects of capital markets having held senior positions at several respected brokerage and investment firms; working with some of the world's largest international funds. Peter's site AlphaVN.com is an independent research and consulting firm focused on southeast Asia where he publishes his views on the capital markets and trading daily. He is a rated broker in Asia Money's Brokers Poll 2012 of fund managers and currently resides in Ho Chi Minh City, Vietnam.

Index

Algorithm, 24, 35, 77, 89, 108, 111–112
   HFT, 111–112
Alpha, 131, 138, 159
Apple (AAPL), 19, 53, 64–69, 79–85, 109, 115, 133, 143, 151–152, 163–167
Asking Price, 43–44, 478, 50, 66
   Lifting Offers, 45, 66, 68, 83, 85
   Volume, 49–50, 61
Auction Market Theory (AMT), 43, 46, 49–50, 61, 67, 84, 138, 154–155, 160
   Fair Value, 14, 43, 46, 84 99, 155
   Market Condition, 43
   Consolidation, 43, 45–47, 50, 84
   Trending, 43–49
   Volume, 46, 49–50, 61

Barnum, P.T., 108
Bayesian Statistics, 92–94
Beta, 160
Bid Price, 42–49, 66, 82, 95, 110
   Hitting Bids, 45–48, 62, 66, 85
   Institutions, 95
   Volume, 96, 99–100
Black-Scholes, 138–139
Bohr, Niels, 20, 23
Breakout, 6, 50–51, 67, 72, 74, 76, 79–81, 85, 87–89, 96, 98–100, 108, 110, 126–127
   Auction Market Theory, 45–49
   Opening Range, 50–51, 74, 85, 87–89
   Trade, 98–100, 163–167
Buffett, Warren, 25

INDEX

Candlestick, 32–33, 52
CAPM, 138
Clarkson, Jeremy, 142
Consolidation, 14, 29, 43, 45–47, 49–52, 61–62, 68, 80, 84, 90, 97–98, 130–132, 134–136, 155, 159–160, 163–165, 167–169, 171
COUNTIF, 66–67, 179–182
Cycles, 38–42, 130, 132–137
    Weekday Effects, 38–42

Data
    Charts, 28, 32, 51, 55
    Histograms, 51, 55–58, 60, 65
    Manipulation, 12, 14–147, 20–22, 31–32, 37–38, 51–58
    Mining, 19–20
    Research, 18–22, 34, 37–42, 51–8, 65
    Statistics, 14–17, 20–22, 38–42, 46, 51–58
Dick, Philip K., 154
Disruptive Technology, 22–23, 122, 148–150
    Internet, 22–23, 148–150
    Mongols, 148–150

Elliott Wave, 9
Europe, 19, 73, 136
Excel, 37, 56, 66, 172–181
    COUNTIF, 66-7, 179–182
    IF, 37

Fair Value, 14, 43, 46, 84, 99, 155
Falsification, 14–17
Federal Reserve, 121, 135
Ford (F), 148–149, 167–171
Ford, Henry, 148–149

Fundamental Analysis, 2, 7, 17–19, 24, 26, 36, 49, 63, 74, 86, 99, 138–141, 144, 152, 155, 159, 172

GDP, 33, 133, 160
Gestalt, 10
Gladwell, Malcolm, 7
Gold, 2, 87, 121
    Sinclair, James, 121
Greece, 36
Greenblatt, Joel, 138–141
Gretzky, Wayne, 141–144

Haiku, 30
High-Frequency Trading, 44, 77, 108, 111, 126
Holmes, Sherlock, 16

I Ching, 145–148
Inside Day, 36–38, 57–58, 61, 78, 120, 160
Implicit Learning, 7, 101–113, 126
Institutional Traders, 35, 39, 53, 61, 95–98, 111, 126
Internet, 22–23, 39, 97, 146–147, 150, 172, 181
    Disruptive Technology, 22–23, 122, 148–150

Jobs, Steve, 4, 25

Level II Quote, 47–49
LG, 19
Lynch, Peter, 25

Mayer, Marissa, 30
Merck (MRK), 27–29
Mongols, 148–150
Music, 31, 36, 92–95, 102, 126

Index

Murphy, John, 14–15
Multistability, 10–17, 160

Newton, Issac, 27
Newtonian Mechanics, 20, 27, 107
Niederhoffer, Victor, 20
Nikkei 225, 2
Nvidia (NVDA), 116–124, 184

Opening Range, 25, 50–55, 62–67, 70–71, 74–75, 77–90, 92, 99, 108, 113–115, 121, 140, 154–155, 159–160, 163–164, 168
   Definitions, 25, 50–55, 62–67
   Breakout, 50–51, 74, 85, 87–89
   Reversals, 98–100, 116–119, 121
   Uses, 70–71, 74–75, 77–90, 113–115, 159–160, 163–164, 168
Opportunity Cost, 18, 140, 144
Optical illusions, 9–17, 22, 107, 110, 160
   Multistability, 10–17, 160
   Penrose Triangle, 13
   Reification, 10–17, 28
Outliers, 7, 11–13, 61, 86
Outside Day, 38, 61, 81, 114, 127, 160

P/E, 29, 132–136, 144, 160
Poker, 3, 21, 24, 31, 116, 140, 142
Popper, Karl, 15
Positivism, 14–17, 26
The Prestige, 6
Psychology, 10–14, 23–24, 108–110, 131, 146
   Gestalt, 10
   Implicit Learning, 7, 101–103, 126

Multistability, 10–17, 160
Popper, Karl, 15
Reification, 10–17, 28

Quantitative Analysis, 8, 23–25

Reasoning, 15–17
Reification, 10–17, 28
Reversals, 51, 57, 79, 98–100, 107–109, 116–109, 121
   Trading, 98–100, 116–119, 121
Rogers, Jim, 137

S&P 500, 37–42, 46, 51, 55, 74, 95, 111, 116, 131–137, 144
Simplicity, 13, 25, 30–31, 63, 73, 107, 154
   Haiku, 30
Sinclair, James, 121
Stop, 40–41, 75, 85, 115–116, 121–122
Statistics
   Analysis, 8, 25, 37–38, 56–59, 65
   Back-testing, 25, 38, 61
   Bayesian, 92
   Building Spreadsheets, 170–178
   Descriptive, 14–15
   Histograms, 51, 55–58, 60, 65
   Inductive, 14–15
   Stock Price, 65, 70–71, 79–83, 87–88, 109, 120–121, 163–175
Subconscious, 73, 91–95, 100
   Bayesian Statistics, 92–94
   Implicit Learning, 7, 101–103, 126

Technical Analysis, 7–18, 26, 28–29, 31, 48–49, 63, 161
   Chart Patterns, 8–13, 16, 102
   Elliott Wave, 9
   Head and Shoulders, 12
   Triangle, 12, 28
   Wedge, 6, 12, 28

INDEX

Trends, 9, 29, 36, 43–49, 51, 55, 61–62, 71–74, 87, 89, 98–99, 108–111, 113, 115–119, 127, 132–134, 160
  Market Condition, 29, 43, 49, 51, 130, 160
  Moves, 43–45, 62, 74, 99, 110, 113, 121, 134
  Macro, 18, 72, 131, 132–134
  Reversal, 110–119
  Trend Length, 46–47, 55, 74, 87, 98, 108, 163 181–183
Trendlines, 9, 28, 34

Unforgiven, 105

Vietnam, 18–19, 42, 102–103, 106, 136, 146–148, 151–152
Valuation Models,
  Black-Scholes, 138–139
  CAPM, 138
  P/E, 29, 132–136, 144, 160
Volatility, 37, 55, 72–3, 97, 109, 121, 127, 131

Alpha, 131, 138, 159
Beta, 160
Volume, 8–10, 16, 25, 29, 31, 35–38, 43–51, 54–85, 61–62, 66–69, 71–72, 76, 79–85, 87–89, 95–99, 100, 109–114, 117, 120, 161
  AMT, 43, 46–49, 61–62
  Analysis, 46-7, 50–51
  Charting, 9, 16, 29,
  Closing, 35–37
  Delta, 47–48, 50, 54, 62, 66–71, 76, 79–82, 85, 89–90, 99, 113, 126, 161
  Opening Range, 52–55
  Volatility, 37

Yahoo! Finance, 2, 14, 29, 39–41, 44, 56, 164, 169, 172, 179
  Data Sourcing, 44, 56, 172, 179, 181,

Zeno's Paradox, 97